A Visit to the Court of Morocco

Arthur Leared

A VISIT TO THE COURT OF MOROCCO

PARDON AND SON, PRINTERS, PATERNOSTER ROW, LONDON.

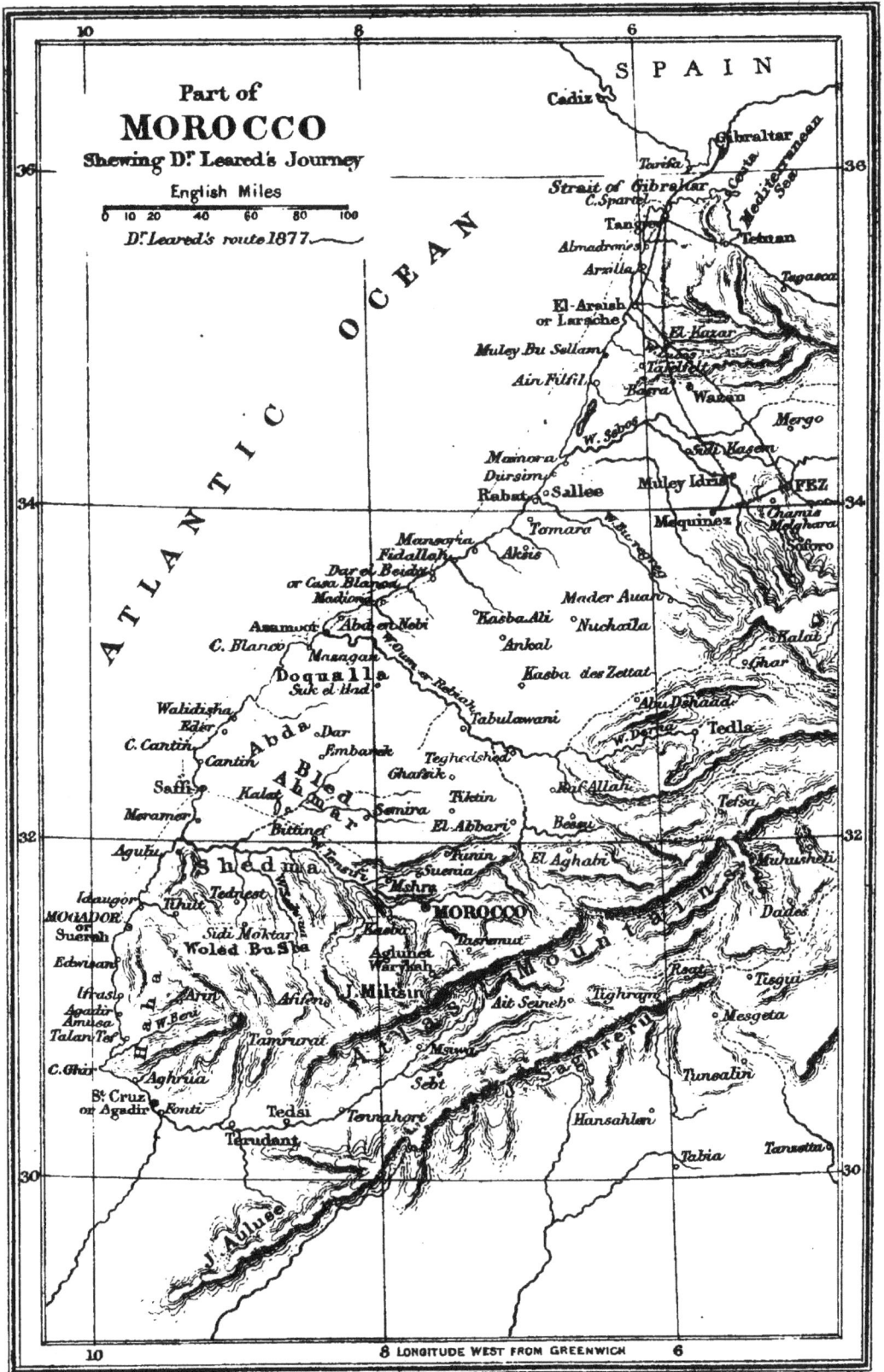

Part of
MOROCCO
Shewing Dr. Leared's Journey

English Miles

0 10 20   40   60   80   100

Dr. Leared's route 1877

S P A I N

A T L A N T I C   O C E A N

Cadiz

Gibraltar
Tarifa
Ceuta
Mediterranean Sea
Strait of Gibraltar
C. Spartel
Tangier
Tetuan
Almadrovis
Arzilla
Tagasca
El-Araish or Larache
El-Kazar
Muley Bu Sellam
Tazrut
Ain Filfil
Basra
Waban
Mergo
Mamora
Sidi Kacem
Dursim
Muley Idris
FEZ
Rabat
Sallee
Mequinez
Chamis Melghara
W. Sebou
Tomara
Safaro
Mansoria
Akais
Fidallah
Dar el Beida or Casa Blanca
Mader Auan
Nuchaila
Kalah
Madiona
Assamur
Abd en Nebi
Kasba Ali
Ankal
Ghar
C. Blanco
Mzagan
Kasba des Zettat
Doqualla
Suk el Had
Abu Dahaad
Walidisha
Tabulawani
W. Derna
Tedla
Edir
C. Cantin
Dar Embarek
Teghedshed
Raf Allah
Tefsa
Cantin
Ghafrik
Saffi
Kalat
Semira
Tiktin
Bessu
Meramer
Bittina
El-Abbari
Agulu
Shedma
Tunin
El Aghabi
Muhasheli
Suenia
Tednest
Mshra
Idaugor
Ihult
MOGADOR or Sueyrah
MOROCCO
Rasenut
Dades
Sidi Moktar
Woled Bu Sba
Kasba
Edwisan
Aglufet Warzhah
Rogi
Tisgui
Ifras
Arul
Afilens
Ait Seireh
Tighra
Mesgeta
Agadir Amslea
W. Beri
Talan Tef
Tamrarat
Msun
Tunoalin
C. Ghir
Aghrua
Sebi
Hansahlan
St Cruz or Agadir
Ronti
Tedsi
Tennahort
Tabia
Tanzetta
Terudant

J. Ailuse

ATLAS MOUNTAINS

Abda
Bled Ahmar
J. Miltsin
Tesrah
W. Oum er Rebiah
White R.
W. Tensift

London, Sampson Low, & Co.

E. Weller, lith.

A VISIT

TO THE

COURT OF MOROCCO

BY

ARTHUR LEARED, M.D. OXON, F.R.C.P.

FELLOW OF THE ROYAL GEOGRAPHICAL SOCIETY, MEMBER OF THE ROYAL IRISH ACADEMY
AND OF THE ICELANDIC LITERARY SOCIETY, COPENHAGEN, ETC., AUTHOR OF
"MOROCCO AND THE MOORS," ETC.

WITH ILLUSTRATIONS

" LET IT SERVE FOR TABLE TALK."—Merchant of Venice.

London:
SAMPSON LOW, MARSTON, SEARLE, & RIVINGTON
CROWN BUILDINGS, 188, FLEET STREET, E.C.
1879

PARDON AND SON, PRINTERS, PATERNOSTER ROW, LONDON.

Dedicated

(BY PERMISSION)

TO

HIS MOST FAITHFUL MAJESTY,

DOM LUIZ I,

KING OF PORTUGAL AND THE ALGARVES.

PREFACE.

———◦◦◦———

THIS little book is founded on a Paper read, in 1878, at the Dublin meeting of the British Association for the Advancement of Science. It consists of a narrative of events in a journey through one of the least-visited parts of the world, and a record of what was seen of a Court and its surroundings, in which pomp and barbarism are strangely blended.

A VISIT TO THE COURT OF MOROCCO.

CHAPTER I.

The Embassy leaves Tangier—The Cavalcade—Alcassar el Kebir —*Lab el Baroud*—A Sacrificial Offering—Passage of the Sebou—A Bride at Home—The Absorbent Properties of Swine — The *Mona* — A Country Governor's Harem— Venomous Snakes—A Grateful Dog—Zacouta—The Lesser Bustard—Another Harem—Doctoring—The Virtues of Seidlitz Powders—Electrifying the Natives—Centipedes —Muley Edris el Kebir—Cassar Pharaon.

THE old proverb said, " It does not fall to the lot of every one to visit Corinth." Neither is it the good fortune of many, as it was mine, to travel with an embassy in Morocco. The opportunity of travelling *en grand seigneur* was the more agreeable because my former journey * was made

* The author had the misfortune to be in the city of Morocco when in revolt against the Government. The people, always hostile to Christians, were in consequence not merely rude, but dangerous. See "Morocco and the Moors," London, 1876.

B

under very different circumstances. By the combination, I have been able to learn more of Moorish life and manners than would have been otherwise possible—and so to my story.

The Embassy of Portugal to congratulate the Sultan on his accession to the throne, of which Senhor Joseph Colaço was the head, was about to proceed to Fez. His wife and daughter, and a niece, were to accompany him. The other members of the Embassy were Senhor Bomtempo, of the Portuguese Foreign Office, who acted as secretary, and was bearer of an order to the Sultan,* Senhor Emanuel de Jesus Colaço, the Ambassador's brother, and Mr. J. Butler, Portuguese vice-consul at Saffi; Mr. C. Murdoch was also of the party. I had the honour to act as physician to the Embassy, and availed myself of the privilege of taking my wife.

On the afternoon of May 21st, 1877, we left the official residence of the Ambassador, and the long procession defiled through the narrow streets of Tangier. It was one of those glorious days of which the delicious climate of that country is prolific, but it must be owned that to European sensations it was too warm. The Embassy had been detained by unavoidable circumstances until the scorching sun had unmistakeably shown that we were about to travel in

---

* Grã Cruz da Torre Espada de Valor lealdade e merito.

a continent over the length and breadth of which he reigns supreme.

First went a party of white-robed Moorish cavalry, headed by a man bearing a large red flag, the emblem of Moorish sovereignty. From its tattered condition, one might have conceived it to have borne the brunt of battle and breeze for at least a century. Several of the ministers and consuls of the various countries, and many other residents of the town, accompanied us for some distance. Outside the town the *cortége* was swollen by a larger body of cavalry. At a little distance it was indeed a gallant and picturesque display. For be it understood once for all, that things Moorish are ill-adapted for præ-Raphaelite investigation. Thus the huge square stirrups and inhuman bridle-bits of our troopers did not shine as they ought to have done in the brilliant sun, nor was there that uniformity in the horses or gloss on their coats that one would look for in one of Her Majesty's cavalry regiments.

Three-and-a-half hours' ride through a fairly cultivated country brought us to a place under a range of hills called Kaa el Urmil, close to the river M'har, where our tents were pitched. One found time here to take stock of the party. First, we were lodged in thirty-five tents, including a large pavilion which formed our dining-room, and we were attended by twenty servants, besides a host of muleteers and others, including one

Portuguese whose business it was to plant the royal standard of Portugal at every encampment in front of the Ambassador's tent. Fifty Moorish cavalry, with a kaid or commander, constituted our permanent guard. Our riding animals numbered thirty, and there were one hundred horses and mules for transport, making a grand total of 128 persons and 180 horses and mules. There were also three camels, which laboured and grunted under the weight of presents designed for His Imperial Highness the Sultan.

Next day, very early, the whole *cortége* was in motion. We advanced for some time close to the sea, and then, having crossed a plain, forded a river about fifty yards wide. Here we were joined by a kaid with a large party of cavalry, and at three hours from starting encamped at the douar of Garbia. There was a long day to be got through here, which was done by shooting the doves which abounded, drinking tea in the kaid's tent, looking at the powder-play of our cavalry while we sipped coffee *al fresco*, or listened to the droning music of a Moorish band.

In less than two hours' journey from this encampment we came upon a magnificent grove of wild olive trees, the massive foliage of which afforded grateful shade from the sun's too powerful glare even in the early morning. It is called by the Moors "the Nightingale wood," from the number of these birds by which it is frequented. Here we were met by the Governor of Larache with a body of about one hundred cavalry, which replaced what may be called the floating portion of our escort. From this place there was a succession of hill and plain with little cultivation; a considerable river was forded, and we stopped at a place called Klatta de Raissana. A disagreeable east wind prevailed during this day.

Out again before sunrise; the long procession once more in motion, now extending more than a mile, now contracting to a third of that dimension, wended its way across a great alluvial plain, through which runs the small river M'Hassen. This is spanned by an ancient stone bridge, and here we stopped to drink to the memory of the gallant, but imprudent, Portuguese monarch, who led his army across this bridge from their strong position into the open plain to be overwhelmed by numbers, and slain almost to a man.*

From the river M'Hassen to Alcassar, a distance of some ten miles, the country was level, yet but little cultivated. A hill was crossed at about two miles from the town, which then came into view. The intervening space was an arid plain, which presented hardly the semblance of any living plant, where nevertheless cattle roamed in search of food.

From the point of view where we encamped,

* See "Appendix A."

Alcassar el Kebir was imposing enough. About a dozen mosque towers, with here and there a few tall palms, and a crowd of flat-roofed houses enclosed within high walls, gave it an air of importance. Outside the walls there were also some fine gardens.

We entered, and all illusion was dispelled. It was market day, and the crowds gathered round our party in the hot, filthy, and dusty streets in a way that was almost unbearable. The shops had no attractions; nothing was to be seen in them except articles of food and clothing. And yet the size and appearance of some of the houses showed that there were citizens of substance in the midst of this squalor. But a general decay was only too plain. Here was to be seen an open space covered with mouldering ruins. There, a minaret, the mosque of which no longer existed. An extraordinary number of storks' nests, perched on towers, on housetops, on old walls and trees, was a feature of the place. Look almost where one would, and one of these big untidy structures met the eye. And sitting in each were two or three ungainly-looking juveniles, over which papa and mamma storks stood gazing at the hopeful but hungry family below.

I judged the town to contain between five and six thousand souls,* and this estimate was con-

* Rohlfs makes the number of inhabitants 30,000. "Adventures in Morocco," London, 1874, page 25.

firmed by the independent statement of a Jew inhabitant. The number of Jews is about 600. The town is more healthy than the neighbouring town of Larache, situated on the sea. Alcassar boasts of no doctor, and yet the people have learned the value of vaccination, which has been introduced from Tangier. By this means the ravages of smallpox, their worst enemy, have been checked.

Every town in Morocco seems to have a legend of its own concerning its origin. The story about the foundation of this town is that the Sultan Mansor, having lost his way on a hunting expedition, was entertained *incognito* by a poor fisherman, in whose hut he passed the night. The Sultan was so well pleased, that he bestowed upon the fisherman some royal buildings, situated not far off. These buildings having been enclosed within a wall, soon took the form of a town, to which the name of Alcassar el Kebir, or, the Great Palace,* was given.

The Ambassador had remained behind to sketch the bridge before-mentioned, and his approach to the camp in the evening was a sight not to be forgotten. He was preceded by a band of native music, and a sharp fusillade was kept up, just as if he were fighting his way to the encampment.

Next morning we passed over about two miles

* "A Geographical History of Africa," by Leo Africanus, translated by John Pory, London, 1600, page 172.

of the best road I had seen in Morocco. It was wide, with a paved footpath, rendered necessary by the soft nature of the ground in the rainy season. This road ended at the ford across the Lucos, here about eighty yards in breadth. Beyond this, the country was better cultivated than usual, and here, May 25th, we saw wheat cut for the first time. Our encampment was in the midst of an immense tract, covered with a fair crop of hay going utterly to waste. It is curious to observe how differently the same article is valued under different circumstances. I had often seen the Icelanders collecting their scanty hay crop—even the sod-covered roofs of their houses being carefully mowed—the only product of their sterile soil and frigid climate. The Moors, on the other hand, never make hay. Climate and soil together confer on them so many other gifts as to render it, at least in their estimation, unnecessary.

During our progress we were honoured every day with the *Lab el Baroud*, or powder-play, by our Moorish guards; when the ground permitted, the performance was almost incessant. It often began before daylight, and as often ended after sunset, when sitting at dinner in our tent. It was a gallant sight to see ten or a dozen Moors charging abreast, their spirited little horses straining nerve and muscle, and apparently enjoying the fun as much as the riders; the robes of the men filled by the breeze, their eyes flashing fire as they whirled and tossed their long guns in the air, and then with one wild, thrilling shout (a prayer to Allah to direct their bullets to the hearts of their enemies), discharging their pieces simultaneously, then checking their horses, and suddenly wheeling round.

This mimic warfare—for in this we have the whole tactics of the Moorish cavalry—is highly inspiriting, and supplies the Moors, both young and old, with an excitement of which they are passionately fond. But to us spectators, the thing, like everything else, became monotonous by repetition. It was only when an accident, such as the following, occurred, that interest in the performance was thoroughly revived, and then the native part of the *cortége* laughed and gibed as only Moors know how. Something tripped up the horse of one of the performers while going full tilt, so that man and beast rolled over like a ball. Marvellous to say, the rider escaped without serious injury, while the horse, having broken loose in the act of being laid hold of, reared and fell over on his back: here was an opportunity for a second explosion of fun not lost by the bystanders. Incidents of this kind were frequent, and kept the Moors in great good humour.

On reaching the bounds of his province, the Governor of Larache, who had accompanied us from Alcassar, left with his escort, which was replaced by a much smaller one, under the command of the son of the Governor of Ben Ouda. His father had taken away the main body of the cavalry to chastise a rebel tribe in the neighbourhood.

We found the Governor's house, to which we were invited, to be a small dilapidated structure, notwithstanding that its owner was reputed wealthy. We were as usual taken into the garden, and regaled with strong green tea. But even this hardly counterbalanced the drowsy tendency induced by the lazy movements, in a circle, of a half-starved mule, and the monotonous creaking of an irrigation wheel hard by, which he turned.

An incident occurred this evening which illustrated very remarkably the habits and tone of mind of this Shemitic race. A theologian would probably have regarded it as proving the ingrained conception in the natural man of the necessity for, and the efficacy of, sacrifice. A Moor, who had, or fancied that he had, experienced some injustice, killed a sheep in front of the Ambassador's tent, and then presented a petition to Senhora Colaço, to the effect that she would intercede with her husband to obtain justice for the suppliant. Moreover, our theologian would not fail to observe that the idea of an intercessor was included in the episode. Amongst the Moors themselves, this slaying of an animal to propitiate the favour of a person in power is a proceeding which never fails to arrest attention. In the present instance the persons appealed to did not care to mix themselves up in a matter about the merits of which they knew nothing.

Next day, however, notwithstanding his previous ill-success, the irrepressible Moor was again to the fore. As the Senhora stepped from her tent in the gray dawn of the morning, there he was kissing the ground at her feet. It was a comical, but at the same time a touching sight, to witness the poor fellow's manœuvres to obtain a hearing.

We crossed the river Guarot by a ford, about fifty yards wide, and then traversed a rolling prairie, covered with short tufty grass, studded with the flowers of a species of chamomile, but without tree or shrub. After a journey of only about ten miles, we stopped at the douar or village of the Governor of the Habassie tribe. The governor excused himself humbly for not doing proper honour by a larger escort to the representative of Portuguese Majesty. It was the old story: the troopers were absent on fighting duty, in which two of their number had just been killed. Once more tea in the Governor's garden, in which were many old acquaintances, such as roses, hollyhocks, larkspurs, and poppies. Next, we were fairly drenched with rose and orange water; this operation was performed with a metal vessel, having a long, narrow spout, by means of which the fluid was poured over one's head and face. After this, a metal censer, with burning charcoal, in which aloe wood was burned, was handed round. The smell was agreeable, but the heat would have been useful if one could have secured it long enough to dry one's wetted clothes.

Our next journey was through so level a tract, that looking westward it had a sea-like horizon. A good deal of this immense expanse was cultivated with wheat and barley, with here and there douars or villages of clustered tents, with a fair number of cattle. But by far the greater part was a fertile waste, waiting in vain for the hand of man to make it productive.

We soon reached the Sebou, one of the principal rivers of Morocco, at this point about 120 yards wide and of considerable depth. Here began a scene of noise and confusion impossible to describe. The passage was effected in rickety, leaky, flat-bottomed boats, into which the camels and many of the horses and mules were partly driven, partly pushed. But the greater number of the animals were made to swim the river by the united yells, reproaches, and blows of a crowd of nearly naked men—now delivered from the bank, now while swimming, or else supported by the tails of the swimming horses and mules. Next the immense heap of baggage piled on the river-bank claimed attention; and altogether the crossing and recrossing, unpacking and packing, occupied four hours' hard work.

In a douar, close to the river's bank on the farther side, was a bride, whom we were allowed to see in her tent. She was undergoing the customary seclusion for a certain number of days. She was young and pretty, and sat almost as motionless as a waxwork—dirty, but bedecked with earrings, with armlets and leglets, and evidently well pleased with herself. Bits of various-coloured silks sewn on to her dress gave her the appearance of a May girl in one of our country villages. There were also running about in this douar a pair of young wild boars. They are kept by the Moors chiefly on account of the absorbent properties attributed to the swine tribe. The notion that they are often beset by evil spirits, is deeply rooted in the Moorish mind. But if there is the bane, there is also the antidote; for it is firmly believed that no devil can resist the attraction of a pig's body as a desirable place of residence; and when so localized, they are presumed to be comparatively harmless. Be that as it may, nothing could well be more impudent, grotesque, and amusing than these prettily-striped little pigs. Gratitude, however, has no place in their character. When nearly grown up, any good conduct they possessed leaves them, and, as in other cases, with it they lose their stripes. After this they become most destructive, if not positively dangerous. Sooner or later, however, it is their invariable practice, no matter what amount of care and attention they have received, to betake themselves and their cargo of devils to their native wilds to be no more seen.

A casual observer might suppose that, in our camp, we had at last lighted upon that prodigal hospitality sometimes attributed to Eastern peoples. Every evening he would see a long train of Moors, some driving sheep, others carrying fowls tied by the legs, others bearing on their heads, trays filled with provisions. One may see the thing exactly represented on certain Egyptian monuments. This daily contribution is called the "mona"; but hospitality, to be genuine, must be voluntary. The offerings were made by order of the Sultan, by whose officers the various villages near which we encamped were compelled to supply all our wants. I could not learn that the people are in any way compensated. "Le roi le veut," and that is enough. The passage of an embassy through the country is, fortunately for the people, not a thing of every-year occurrence. This day's allowance consisted of six sheep (on some occasions it had been ten), a calf, thirty fowls, eight loaves of sugar, eight packets of candles, a large quantity of bread, butter, and oranges, besides barley for the animals.

Our next journey was over a flat fertile country, having some splendid wheat crops, and

through great tracts, as thickly covered with a
tall white-flowering umbelliferous weed as if
cultivated. This weed must impoverish the ground
sadly, and its only earthly use is that the Moors
make toothpicks out of the little stalks which
go to form the umbel. The escort, which met
us soon after our departure, amounted to 168
horsemen, and we had powder play all the way
in great perfection. We encamped on the bank
of the river Irrdrum, a tributary of the Sebou,
on a dead level plain, having to the south a fine
amphitheatre-like range of distant hills. Close
at hand was the village of Bokhara, where the
Governor of the Shaarda tribe's house was situated.

Our progress had hitherto been, in all con-
science, slow enough, and yet here the Ambassador received the salutations of the Sultan with
a request that we should not hurry. His Majesty
also sent word that he would receive us at Mequinez
instead of at Fez, where we intended going. We
remained at this place in consequence two days.

The Governor's house here was of the same
class as others already described: no glass in the
windows, no paint on the tin-bound doors and
shutters. Our ladies were invited into the harem,
which presented a sight the reverse of imposing.

In a court surrounded by apartments, about
thirty women, white and black, were huddled
together. Some of the commoner sort were shel-
tered in a camel's-hair tent in the middle of the

enclosure. The women were described as fat and dirty, and, with few exceptions, not pretty. No end of stark-naked children were running about or else in their mothers' arms.

The old Governor consulted me about his health; he was weak, he said, and required a strong tonic. Outside the house was a large matamore, or excavation in the earth for storing corn. It had not been used for years, and a few days before our arrival, three men went down for the purpose of putting it in repair. They were bitten by a deadly species of viper, called by the Moors *el effa* (translated, the violent-tempered), and all three died almost immediately. These vipers frequent places of this kind.

I cannot resist telling a story here of which a dog is the hero. Nilo, a Spanish pointer, belonging to the Ambassador, had his leg broken by the fall upon it of a tent pole. The poor animal suffered terribly, and the question was what was to be done with him. The prevailing opinion was that he ought to be put out of pain by a speedy death. However, by the aid of Mr. Murdoch, I managed to set his limb, and a black man was told off to look after the patient. That evening the cries of the dog again became distressing. I found poor Nilo in a deplorable state, his broken leg having got twisted while his negro nurse lay beside him in a profound stupor from the effects of smoking kief, or Indian hemp.

Some Moors who were with me shouted to the sleeper in a way that might wake the dead. But Hadge em Bark was insensible to everything until his head was lifted up by one of his ears. Then for an instant there was a diabolical grin, and again his features were as still as death. When philanthropists have succeeded in suppressing alcohol and its effects, they should turn attention to hemp, which ignominiously destroys life in more ways than one. Once more I succeeded in preventing Nilo from being killed on the score of putting him out of pain. The dog was ultimately left behind in care of a Moor, who was to be paid on our receiving the animal on the return journey.

Some weeks afterwards the same dissipated negro was dispatched to bring the animal to our camp, as we did not return by the same route. My persistent efforts to make friends with the dog previous to his accident had utterly failed. He was sullen and indifferent. But the moment Nilo, now nearly well, was released from the mule's back on which he had been brought into camp, he came and seated himself in my tent, wagging his tail, looking at me as if he wanted to say, as I have no doubt he felt, "I am very grateful to you, and I have come to see you first." From that time, Nilo and I were great friends. One is tempted to say with the French cynic, "Plus je connais les hommes, plus j'admire les chiens."

About four miles from this encampment, hilly country commenced. But from the bridge, over the M'Hassen to this point, a distance of about seventy miles, the country was so level that a splendid road might be made at a comparatively small cost. After having crested the hills and made a short descent, we arrived at our stopping place, by name Zacouta. Here, by direction of the Sultan, we were obliged to delay five days. His Majesty's progress is always slow, and the short journey on which he was then engaged, namely, going from Fez to Mequinez, occupied many days. He was anxious that our *cortége* should not come in contact with the Imperial host, to feed which must have sorely taxed the resources of the country through which it passed.

We had plenty of time for investigation in this disagreeable place. Our camp was on flat, parched soil, deeply fissured by the summer heat which was now felt in all its fierceness. The thermometer in our tent, a roomy Moorish one, oval in shape, and lined with stout woollen cloth, reached 99°F. On one night we had a thunderstorm with rain, but it afforded us little or no relief.

We found that the lesser bustard, called by the Moors *rad*, a fine game bird not known near the coast, was plentiful here. It is about the size of a pheasant, but plumper, and flies in coveys. We tried to shoot them, but the heat even in the early mornings, the wildness of the birds, and the want of dogs, made us unsuccessful. On one of our excursions, I found with some reapers a young *rad* tethered by the leg, and this bird, which was easily tamed, proved for some time afterwards an amusing pet, until it was allowed to starve by the Moor who had it in charge.

Our encampments were generally so arranged as to be near the residence of the governor of the tribe in whose district we travelled. In this part of the country these residences were small and poor-looking, contrasting remarkably with the huge piles of unbaked earthen walls with extensive courtyards belonging to the governors in Southern Morocco. The house of the great man of Zacouta was no exception. Here it was my fortune, or misfortune, to be admitted into the recesses of the harem to prescribe for a patient. A dirtier, plainer set of women it would be difficult to find. The only thing that could be said for them was that they were fat; but in the eyes of a Moor, fatness is a cloak which covers a multitude of faults.

This leads me to speak of my peculiar troubles in the professional line. It is well known that in the East every Frank is supposed to possess an intuitive knowledge of the healing art. In Morocco the same delusion prevails. And when a man has the misfortune to be known as a real *tabib*, as the Moors call a doctor, let him expect no respite. At every stopping-place there

were no end of patients, and when stationary
for some days, one's practice increased immensely.
Some were fever-stricken, others loathsome from
skin diseases : the lame, the blind, the deaf, the
childless, and the lean—for the last two were
conditions for which remedies were eagerly sought
—all thronged round our tent.   Mention has
already been made of the method of intercession
in obtaining favours, and in the present instance
it came largely into play.   The *tabib* himself was
seldom asked or even thanked for his services ;
but the *tabib's* wife was constantly knelt to, and
had her clothes kissed, to induce her to obtain the
good offices of her husband.

It is needless to say that I tried to help
the poor creatures as far as the limited resources
of my medicine chest allowed.   I was particularly indebted to Senhor Emmanuel Colaço and to
Messrs. Murdoch and Butler, without whose aid
as interpreters and in many other ways it would
have been impossible for me to have done anything.   But the demands of the patients were
both incessant and exorbitant.   The Moor im-
plicitly believes that the European doctor *can*
cure him, and that if he does not, it is only
because he will not.   Moreover, the patient brooks
no delay.   He expects an immediate cure.   This,
to say the least, was not a little awkward, and
led to much disappointment.

It can hardly then be wondered at that one

was induced to try various devices with no higher
object in view than that of making an impression.
These devices took different forms, and a few of
them are here given for the benefit of future
travellers.

One of my great resources was a box of Seidlitz powders, and it also afforded much amuse-
ment. Who could help laughing at the sight
of a great dark Othello, invariably drawing back
through fear of being scalded, when the effer-
vescing draught was presented to him? It was
never swallowed, indeed, until the recipient had
first ascertained by a hasty dip of his finger that
the liquid was not boiling over by some cold
process known to the Satan-leagued Christians.

In many instances, however, the Seidlitz
powders were administered by an altogether new
method. The Moors believe in what is profes-
sionally termed heroic treatment; that is to say, in
that which acts strongly and with no possibility of
mistake about effect. Now every one knows that
Seidlitz powders are composed of acid and alkali,
and that to make them effervesce properly, it is
necessary to dissolve one of each in separate
portions of water, and then to mix them. It
occurred to me, that if the patient were to
swallow these solutions separately and in quick
succession, an imposing effect might be produced.
Indeed, the result exceeded all expectation. The
sudden but harmless distension caused by the

internal gaseous evolution was usually succeeded
by an indescribable look of alarm, followed by pres-
sure of the hands upon the stomach, while a pious
Ma-shal-lah ("God is great") ejaculated slowly
but with much fervour, was almost overwhelmed
by the furious rush of imprisoned gas.   It was
currently believed that the devil had to do
with this matter also, and it was more than pro-
bable that the internal commotion and manifest
escape of something invisible were set down to
the palpable expulsion of an evil spirit.

This remedy was held to be potential not only
against immaterial beings, but against substances
as heavy as lead.   Men with gunshot wounds
received in their tribal fights, not infrequently
required assistance.   A warrior, who had a
bullet lodged in his back, appeared one morning,
bringing a basket of figs in gratitude for his
successful treatment.   This consisted of a Seidlitz
powder, which he felt satisfied had moved the
bullet considerably.   Another resource of the
healing art was made to serve an ignoble but
very laughable purpose.   Mr. Butler brought
with him a small electro-magnetic apparatus.   It
was great fun to observe the look of blank
astonishment on their faces, when the electric
current was passed through the bodies and
arms of a lot of Moors seated in a circle.
But a plan we adopted of testing the endurance
of Moors and Jews *versus* their cupidity afforded

the most ludicrous sight imaginable. First, be
it remembered, that a dollar was a sum to secure
which most of them would endure almost any
amount of pain. The conditions, then, were to
hold in the hand one handle of the battery while
the other handle was placed in a basin of water,
at the bottom of which, within temptingly easy
reach, lay the silver prize. The poor fellow's
immersed hand was of course provokingly closed
by an uncontrollable spasm, while his face was
as invariably contorted in a manner that sent the
bystanders into roars of laughter. The mirth of
their own countrymen was indeed perfectly up-
roarious. This game was often repeated, and in
no single instance was the prize legitimately
gained. Any attempt to explain the process by
which the results in this case were obtained was
simply hopeless. We therefore allowed judgment
to go by default, and that judgment was that
the strange effects in this case also were due to
the direct agency of Shaitan, or the evil one,
the Mohammedan representative of the Christian's
devil.

The only thing good at this encampment was
the water, but the excessive heat, and probably
the nature of the ground, were fast bringing ill-
ness into our camp. Another inconvenience connected with the heat was the increased activity and
fierceness of the insect world. The mosquitoes were
bloodthirsty to the last degree; every creeping

thing seemed now to move with tenfold .vigour, and amongst them were creatures the like of which even those accustomed to the country had never seen before.

Senhor Colaço, while sitting in his tent, felt something cold touching his neck, which he at first supposed to be the leather strap of his cap. He was horrified on putting up his hand to find a huge centipede twined under his chin, but he most fortunately escaped being bitten. After that we saw several of these black monsters, which measured about eight or nine inches in length, both in and out of the tents. When disturbed they invariably dived into the heat cracks in the earth.

At last, on the 5th of June, we left Zacouta, by no means deeply regretted by the inhabitants, who were obliged to provide gratuitously for so many mouths. The road lay through a succession of hills, on the slopes of which was much standing corn. After a short journey, we camped under the mountain of Zarhoun, on the southern side of which, less than a mile distant, was the town and sanctuary of Muley Edris el Kebir. The shrine of this holy man, who was the father of the founder of Fez, is regarded throughout Morocco with peculiar veneration. No Christian is ever allowed to enter the town in which it is placed. On the day before our arrival, the Sultan, on his way to Mequinez, visited the sanctuary, according to custom. On our right, across a stream with deep banks, and on higher

ground, stood the ruins called Cassar Pharaon. As
so little was known about these interesting ruins,
the opportunity was taken of examining them carefully, the result of which will be found elsewhere.*
Antiquarian pursuits were conducted here under
difficulties. The thermometer stood in the tents at
102° F., and at this temperature one's energies
begin to flag.

Cassar Pharaon is about 12 miles from Mequinez,
and we made a short journey in the afternoon of the
following day; first over hills, from which at last
the city came into view, and then across a large
plain. Here we were met by a great body of
cavalry, and powder play was conducted on the
most extensive scale. We had been expected in
the early morning, and the men had had no food all
day; but that seemed to make no difference with
these hardy horsemen. We camped for the night
close to the Wad Cazar (river of trees).

* See " Appendix B."

CHAPTER II.

NEXT morning all were astir betimes for our final
advance towards the city, now distant about six
miles. A detour was, however, made, in order to
enter by a particular gate. We were enveloped in
a perfect cloud of horsemen firing their guns, and
dashing about in such a strange manner as to suggest an equestrian form of insanity, and that " Colney
Hatch Prancers " would be a good name for these
erratic troops. That there was some method in the

madness was shown, however, by the flags, thirty-
one of which were counted, each indicating the head
of a tribe, and being the rallying point of a separate
body of cavalry.

Three of the Sultan's brothers, young men, distinguished by the fineness and snowy whiteness of
their flowing robes and their splendid horses, soon
joined the procession. The Prime Minister, the
Commander-in-Chief, and other high officials, accompanied the princes. Next we entered between two
lines of infantry, which extended from the gate into
the plain for a distance judged to be about three-
quarters of a mile. As these troops stood close
together, their numbers must have been very considerable. They consisted chiefly of askars, or
soldiers of the Sultan's guard, dressed with some
regard to uniformity in Fez caps, red flannel jackets,
and vests ; and of other troops, that seemed to have
appropriated the cast-off uniforms of every army
under the sun. The arms of all were either old
flint or percussion muskets.

As we passed through the long lines there was a
great din of drums, and a brass band discoursed
unknown music. Everywhere there was a clash
and clang, and barbaric pomp, to signalize our
approach to the clay-built walls, huge as sombre, of
the imperial city.

It was remarked that our reception by the Moorish authorities was unusually demonstrative. The
Ambassador, long resident amongst them, was very

popular with the Moors; and between the realm
of Portugal and the Sultanate of Morocco there has
long existed a cordiality which contrasts strongly
with the relations between Spain and Morocco.
No longer aggressive, Portugal is content with
the memories of her valiant exploits on Moorish
soil, as well as in more distant regions. The old
feuds are forgotten, and the flag of Portugal is
always received with honour and respect.

The guest house of the Sultan, to which we
were conducted, situated in a blind street near
the great Mosque, El Kebir Cubith Sook, was in
fair repair for a Moorish building. The open-air
central tiled space or patio, in which was a fountain that constantly played, was 35 feet square.
A lofty room ten feet wide opened on each side
into the patio. These rooms had no windows, and
the weather being hot, the large arched doorways
were only closed by curtains. On the floor above,
rooms, the counterparts of those below, opened on
to a wide wooden balcony. It was, in fact, an
eight-roomed house, having attached to it some
small dark rooms for kitchen, bath rooms, &c.
The stone stairs resembled those found in medi-
æval castles, in their narrowness and steepness.
The rooms were simply whitewashed, and without
decoration, except that the lower part of the sides
of the doorways was covered with tiles arranged
in patterns. We had iron bedsteads, and some
rooms, in addition to the divan or sofa, boasted of

a chair. It was curious to observe pieces of English carpets usurping the places of the more appropriate and more handsome Moorish rugs.

As there are no milestones in Morocco, and no surveys have been made, I took pains to ascertain the distance travelled. Taking the walking pace of a mule at four miles an hour, and carefully allowing for stoppages, I arrived at the conclusion that Mequinez is 157 miles from Tangier by the road we travelled.* Such was our slow progress, that eighteen days were consumed in accomplishing the journey.

Mequinez is a more modern-looking city than Fez, with wider streets. It is the sacerdotal city of the empire, and contains many large mosques and seminaries. Its high walls, with towers at about two hundred paces distance from each other, and huge gates, some of them very handsome, gave it somewhat of a defiant aspect. The walls were made of a compound of lime and sun-dried clay, disfigured, as all such walls are in Morocco, by a number of square holes, which might be taken for loopholes for musketry. These holes are caused by the insertion of pieces of timber in building the wall, by a process to be afterwards described. The filling of these holes falls out after a time, and nesting places for birds are thus formed. Owing to this, an amazing number of hawks, jays, and pigeons, all

* See "Appendix D."

appearing to live on perfectly friendly terms, were flushed when one went round the walls. The outside circuit of the walls seemed about five miles, and the number of inhabitants was set down by an intelligent Moor at 25,000. It was evidently formerly much larger, as so far from there being any appearance of tension from want of building room, there were many gardens and ruins within the walls. And, although we traversed the city in all directions, I saw only one house in course of erection, and that was in the Mellagh, or Jews' quarter.

In the eyes of the Moors, Mequinez, and all that belongs to it, are regarded as perfection. The mere mention of the place causes them at times to lift one shoulder in an expressive way, accompanying the act with what may be called a whistle in a whisper, as who would say, "Ah, I believe you; that *is* the place." The women of the city are regarded as the handsomest in Morocco, and the term "Mequinesia" applied to any woman is looked on as a great compliment. The political power, trade, and vastness of Fez, are duly lauded, but Mequinez is the seat of learning, which means of theology. A great number of the inhabitants are connected with the court, or else with the army.

The second day after our arrival, we went by invitation to dine at the house of the Vizier, or Prime Minister, Sid Moosa Ben Hamed, an elderly, acute, pleasant-faced man, of very courteous manners. We were entertained in a room opening on to a fine garden, with fountains and terraces kept in good order. Our host, with some of his friends, did the honours well, without partaking of the feast. A Lord Mayor's dinner could hardly compete with this in number and variety of dishes. The meat and poultry dishes for our small party numbered thirty, the salads twelve, and the sweetmeats thirty-two; but there was no dessert, and of course no wine. The ladies were admitted afterwards into the harem, where they saw a crowd of fifty or sixty women, varying from twelve or thirteen to fifty years of age; two of the great man's wives were as fat as the fattest creatures ever seen at a cattle show. The children were reported as beyond counting.

Our ladies had several other opportunities of knowing all about this harem. The entrance was always guarded by black slaves, creatures hardly to be called men. The Sid's legal wives were always courteous and pleasant. Each had her own department in housekeeping, such as cooking, washing, cleaning, &c., and they evidently possessed extensive powers over the other women. All the women were polite, although inquisitive; their questions were confined to the very few subjects suggested by their limited experience of life. Ornaments, dress (this was also very practically examined into), health, babies, and husbands, formed the chief points of discussion. The smallness of our ladies' waists, compared with their own, made them laugh immoderately. The sight of Europeans was an event in their monotonous lives. It is believed that, with the exception of two daughters of Sir J. D. Hay, no English, probably no European women, had been seen at Mequinez in recent times.

Four days after our arrival, the grand event of the journey, our public reception by the Sultan, took place. At eight o'clock in the morning we rode, through a gateway of noble proportions, into a large quadrangular enclosure of the palace, surrounded by high walls. From that we passed into a similar enclosure, and finally into a third, about three acres in extent. Soldiers standing closely together lined the walls of these great spaces. Having dismounted from our horses, we were arranged by the M'Chouar, or master of the ceremonies, opposite to a large gateway. The Ambassador, Senhor Bomtempo, and Mr. Butler, were in official uniforms. Just behind us five mules stood in a row, laden with the presents from the monarch of Portugal to his Moorish brother.

Presently there was a blast of trumpets, and the great wooden gate was suddenly thrown open, and from it issued five magnificent led horses, gaily caparisoned, and bearing themselves as if conscious of the dignity of the occasion.

But the step from the sublime downwards is often abrupt. Next came forth a one-horse chaise driven by a man on foot, there being no driving seat.

The horse was harnessed a long way from the little yellow vehicle. Where this could have originally come from, it would be difficult to say. One must suppose that as no one drives a carriage in Morocco, it was intended to typify the might and grandeur of its august owner, whom it immediately preceded.

The Sultan now made his appearance, mounted on a splendid grey horse. A man with a bright spear gleaming in the sunlight walked at each side of his charger. Behind the spearman on the right walked an attendant bearing a large red umbrella with a golden knob on the top of its long handle, with which his Sharifian Majesty's face was carefully shaded. Two other attendants, with white silk handkerchiefs in their hands, seemed to be assiduously dusting both horse and rider, but the meaning of this was that the troublesome flies were no respecters of persons.

At the instant the Sultan came in view, every soldier present bowed almost to the ground, and shouted at the top of his voice, " *Allah bark amar Sidna* " ("The blessing of God fill our Lord.") Twice was this shouting and bowing repeated. The effect was really grand; turn where one would, hundreds of dusky faces were seen bending downwards in trained obedience, while the blended clamour of many thousand throats almost persuaded one that the object of so much devotion must be more than mortal. Anything more impressive it would not be easy to find.

D

We now approached close, and stood face to face with His Majesty, or more correctly speaking, with his horse. The Ambassador then read an address and handed it to the Sultan, who handed it to his Prime Minister, standing with other high officials in close attendance. Some complimentary words were now exchanged through the medium of Mr. Butler, and then the Ambassador presented us each in turn to the Sultan. Mr. Murdoch, although present unofficially, received a special recognition. His name was well known to His Majesty as one of the principal merchants trading in his dominions. The reception did not occupy more than a quarter of an hour. When it was over, His Majesty, attended by his spearmen, his umbrella-bearer, and his fly-flappers, rode leisurely away through a different gate from that by which he entered. And now came the clang of Moorish music, and the uproar of five fieldpieces rapidly discharged, while the report of each was tripled by echoes from the surrounding walls. Moreover, the soldiers, no longer under restraint, added to the noise and confusion. It was a very chaos of disorder.

The ladies, mounted on their mules, witnessed the reception at a distance of about twenty yards, and it was observed that the royal eyes frequently wandered in their direction.

The Sultan, Hassan Ben Mohammed, seemed to be about forty years of age. He was tall, and of good presence. His complexion was pale and his features expressive. He gave the impression of energy and mental power. He was dressed in the usual white haic, with light blue underclothing. The horse-trappings were green-coloured, and embroidered with gold.

After the reception, we were taken to see various things connected with the royal establishment. We saw the Sultan's horses, to the number of between thirty and forty, tethered in a large yard exposed to the rays of the burning sun. Many of them were splendid animals, showing much breeding, and some were decidedly vicious. All the horses in Morocco are stallions, but the stranger must not expect to find amongst them a preponderance of fine animals. The Barb horse has a good reputation; but the truth is, most of the Moorish horses are poor mongrels, small and ill-shaped, but hardy and serviceable. Those of the right sort are highly valued, and consequently by no means easy to obtain.

We passed through two of the royal gardens, which, except in extent, differed little from others we had seen. They were orchards rather than gardens, in which were apple and pear, plum, peach, and cherry, orange, lemon, citron, pomegranate, almond, and other trees, besides vines, and a few common flowers. As the ground was well irrigated, all these grew in great luxuriance. Fairly-well-kept walks divided the grounds, and some of them led up to summer

houses, decorated with tiles and arabesque ceiling
decorations. In one of the summer houses was
a velvet-covered French sofa.

We were also shown a large park-like enclosure,
in which a number of ostriches were confined,
and where they bred—an ostrich farm, in fact.
The birds were very shy, and they had for
companions, gazelles as wild as themselves, and
also camels and horses.

Our reception by the Sultan, as might be
supposed, caused us to be honoured by invitations from high officials. Sid Abdallah Ben
Hamed, Governor of Fez, Sid Moosa's brother,
entertained us handsomely. Our host was a small
man about seventy years of age, showing more
negro blood than his brother, to whom he was
said to be greatly inferior in ability. He received us in an octagon room measuring about
twenty-five feet from side to side, with a lofty
green-painted ceiling, and green-and-white tiled
floor spread with rich carpets. One side of this
apartment opened by a door into a long narrow
room, while the counterpart of this door and
room were placed exactly opposite. On the floor
of one of these outer rooms were squatted fourteen fat and sleek ulemas of the highest rank;
gentlemen who combined the somewhat incon-
gruous professions of law and divinity. Amongst
them were some fine faces; that of a personage,
whose post corresponded with that of our Lord

Chief Justice, was particularly striking.   But truth to say, what with the heat, the monotony of the music intended to entertain us, and of looking at wretched Franks feeding—all this combined intellect of the land was soon unconscious of our presence.   In a word, the magnates fell asleep!   In the opposite room, a number of merchants, chiefly from Fez, were congregated. Invitations had evidently been given to all these notables by our host, to come and see the Christians then on view.

This time we had napkins, plated forks, and German painted tumblers, but the only thing provided to put into the latter was tepid water. All the time of dinner—about an hour—we had to endure the noise of four singers and players on a kind of fiddle and tambourine.   The viands and sweetmeats were much the same as at the Prime Minister's.

We also dined at the Grand Chamberlain's, Hadge Mahomed Ben Aish, a burly, big-featured, but good-natured looking man.   He entertained us in a room opening on to a really nice garden, laid out with tiled walks, tanks, and a fountain. Our dinner service was the old willow pattern; the forks, the old steel ones.   The apartment was handsomely decorated in the Moorish style, but spoiled by articles from Europe.   There were great bunches of tawdry artificial flowers under tall glass shades on shelves at each end of the room; two moderate-sized mirrors in gold frames, and, most objectionable of all, four clocks, two smaller French ones, and two larger, all ticking away. In another room were two other clocks. Our host's passion for clocks was very remarkable.

The commandant of the soldiers who accompanied us from Tangier, Kaîd Mehedi, lived at Mequinez, and his invitation could not be refused. Here there was no taint of Europe. He gave us baked mutton, fowls, and kuscussoo, which we consumed in true Moorish style, without knife or fork, using only the right hand, an awkward proceeding for a novice, but in accordance with etiquette. The upper room in which we dined looked into a small patio below, and here the gimberi and tom-tom players were placed, and also a dancer and clever contortionist. One of his performances was very curious: while standing he bent his body backwards so as to pick with his eyelids a pin out of a handkerchief on the ground. A whole crowd of veiled women and children looked down on these performances from the roof of the house. One wondered where they could have come from, but it soon appeared that the inmates of neighbouring harems had, according to custom, climbed from their own roofs, attracted by the chance of a little excitement in the dull routine of their lives.

One more Moorish feast must be mentioned.

Although not honouring us by his presence, the Sultan entertained us right royally. It was at a summer house in the Basha's garden, where the *chef* of the palace was sent to superintend the proceedings. The numerous dishes were heated on the spot, and all agreed that the royal cooks understood the mystery of flavours, and especially the management of garlic, in perfection.

We were also feasted by some of the rich Jews, and visited many of their houses. Here we were of course allowed to see the women, and the conclusion arrived at was that the daughters of Israel did not share equally in the alleged charms of the veiled beauties of Mequinez. Few of the Jewesses were handsome; they were in general fat and flabby. In one house we saw a married lady nine years of age, the husband being thirteen; they were, as well they might be, a very shy couple, and tried to avoid observation.

The condition of the Jews at Mequinez and Fez is much the same as it is in the city of Morocco, elsewhere fully described.* In the midst of insult and bad treatment, they manage to exist, and a few of them to become rich. It was painful to see the manner in which our guards ill-treated any unfortunate Israelite that happened to press upon us in our progress through

* *See* " Morocco and the Moors," page 179.

the streets. One poor wretch was thrown down with such violence that his shoulder-bone was broken. A small sum of money subscribed between us quite consoled him for the injury. Probably a similar sum would have compensated him for the like injury to the other shoulder. It is curious, however, how tyranny makes tyrants. We could not fail to observe that in their own quarter the headmen of the Jewish community knocked the populace about almost in the same way.

One day a request came through the Prime Minister that I should go in a professional capacity to the Sultan's palace. As this gave me the rare opportunity of visiting the interior of this huge place, I shall describe what I saw. Mr. Butler was allowed to accompany me as interpreter.

We entered by the same gate as when received by the Sultan, and passing, as before, through different enclosures, were led into a wide straight street, at least one-third of a mile in length. At each side were solid walls of sun-dried clay, about five-and-thirty feet in height. It looked like a yard in Newgate indefinitely prolonged. In one of the walls were small doorways which opened into public offices, and around these doorways were crowds of men and horses. Passing through one of these doors, we found ourselves in a small courtyard, and from that

we were ushered into a dark apartment. The
state of things here was extraordinary; on one
side were bales and boxes of goods piled up to
the vaulted roof, others were scattered about,
and on some of these we were invited to seat
ourselves. One side of the room was, however,
less encumbered, and here, on a narrow strip
of carpet, placed close to the walls, sat several
greybearded, grave personages. Before each was
a box and a little unpainted desk, and all were
writing or counting money. These were high
officials, transacting business connected with the
state. One was the Commander-in-Chief of the
askars, another the head of the treasury, and so
on. Another cellar-like room on the opposite
side of the courtyard was the office of the Prime
Minister himself, and we were told that he
sometimes preferred transacting business seated
on a carpet spread in the open court. There
was a rough-and-ready crudeness, with a dash
of barbarism, about the whole thing, that was
refreshing. To realize the situation, the Duke
of Cambridge and Sir Stafford Northcote must
be imagined seated on the floor of a dark room,
say, in the Custom House, crowded with merchandise, and Lord Beaconsfield squatted on a
rug in a cellar, or in Palace Yard, while con-
ducting the important business of their respec-
tive departments!

We had sufficient opportunity to take in all the

surroundings here, and time was beginning to drag slowly, when we were again conducted into the broad avenue, and almost to its further extremity. Ranged along one of the high walls were a large number of marble pillars, in pieces of about five feet long by three in diameter. The Ionic capitals were collected in another place. These pillars were said to have belonged to a part of the palace erected by Muley Ishmael, now in ruins, and to have been brought from Leghorn. It is difficult to imagine how they could have been conveyed from the coast. The Sultan Muley Sliman greatly enlarged the palace, which was built more than a century and a-half ago by Muley Ishmael. The building, with its green tiled roof, which contained the tomb of Muley Sliman, was a conspicuous object within the palace enclosure. Everything grand was attributed to this potentate.

From the great avenue, we entered another high-walled enclosure, in part lined by a piazza. In the open space stood a little mosque within a kind of yard. There was now a great discussion about the admission of Christians within the precincts of a mosque, which was cut short by the officer who conducted us, saying that the Sultan commanded it. Here in a small lodge attached to the mosque lay the object of my visit; not a patient, as expected, but a corpse. It was that of a young negro girl about whose death suspicion of foul play had arisen.

All that I could learn was that she had been an inmate of the harem, and although in her usual health that morning, died suddenly about noon. Two women at my request lifted the body out of the little dark hut, and placed it on the ground under the shade of a trellised vine. I was requested to observe whether there were marks of strangulation or other violence, which were negatived, and to say whether death was caused by poison; but from a superficial examination of the body no reply could be made to this question. The Moors maintained, on the contrary, that inspection of the tongue would enable me to settle the point, even to the extent of saying what particular poison had destroyed life. This knowledge, although thrust upon me, I did not choose to claim. Meantime Mr. Butler counselled prudence in speech, lest some innocent wretch might lose a head in the matter before sunset. Silence is golden in such a case, and I got out of the difficulty by promising a written statement, which was afterwards handed to Sid Moosa to be translated for the Sultan's consideration.

The Maghasen, or palace enclosure, at Mequinez was of square shape, and about a mile across. It was placed in the south of the town, and included gardens, and also in its south angle a square tank, about four acres in extent. Spaces, some the size of large London squares, surrounded by high walls, one opening into the other as already described, gave the impression of a prison on a gigantic scale.

There was no palatial pile of buildings in our sense of the words. A number of long narrow rooms, sometimes quite isolated, formed the chief apartments. There were also a good many square or oblong rooms, with sloping green-tiled roofs. These served for reception rooms, storehouses, and other purposes.

It may be asked what the Moors seemed to think or say about the war then raging, in which their co-religionists were so hardly pressed by the Russians. The answer is, nothing at all. The Ambassador had a long private interview with the Sultan in one of his garden houses, during which His Majesty never alluded to the subject. In the many interviews which we had with the Prime Minister the subject was only once touched on in a casual way. For this there are several reasons. The Stamboul Sultan is not regarded by the Moors as the head of their religion. In a certain sense, they may be looked on as Protestants; their own sovereign is the head of their Church, and not the potentate whose religious sway, like the Pope's, extends over various nation-alities. Between Turk and Moor there is, there-fore, no political tie. Moreover, the policy of the Moorish government is that of isolation. As regards the outer world, their motto is, "Let us alone and we shall leave you alone." And without doubt it is a sensible policy. They instinctively feel that, as they are so much behind other nations, and are unable to cope with them in arms, independence lies in isolation. When told of European progress and improvements, they reply that these things are suited for others but not for them. And with the example of Turkey before them, it does seem that in these matters there is no middle way of safety. If, like the Japanese, the Moors adopted the policy along with the arts of Europe, they might take their place among the nations as a strong State. But against this course their religion presents an insuperable barrier.

At Alcassar, a native of Algiers who spoke French, visited us. He said he was an envoy from Turkey to the Sultan of Morocco to ask for assistance against Russia. He told us he was then employed in trying to excite the people by religious enthusiasm. But he seemed to succeed very badly, and we much doubted whether he was really accredited by the Porte.

A guard of twenty askars with an officer always stood or squatted in the street outside the door of the Embassy. It was kindly arranged by the Ambassador that we could at any time obtain an escort for our many walks and rides. All went off smoothly except on one occasion, when I ventured with my wife through the great open space in the city at a time when it was filled with the scum of the populace witnessing powder-play and other games in honour of the wedding of the Prime Minister's son. We were scowled at and hooted; the presence of infidels seemed, in fact, to have a

very disturbing effect upon the lighter moments of
the followers of the Prophet. Our guards closed
round, the captain drew his sword and looked fierce,
and we were fortunately soon extricated from the
excited crowd through a gate which led outside the
town walls. It was then noticed that a mounted
man followed us closely, although warned off, and
moreover, that he more than once aimed at my wife
with his long gun. Three of our guards now rushing upon him, instantly dragged him from his horse,
and deprived him of his weapon. The matter was
afterwards hushed up, so that we never could ascertain what punishment the man received, whether the
gun was loaded or whether it was returned to him.
The probability was that the askars extracted a fine
from the man on their own account as the price of
not putting the matter in the hands of the higher
authorities.

Some days after our public reception by the
Sultan, a procession, headed by an official, arrived
from the palace with presents, all methodically
ticketed, for the various members of the Embassy.
Besides other articles, the Ambassador was presented
with a magnificent black horse and his trappings,
the saddle of huge dimensions, its cover of green
velvet encrusted with gold embroidery, with fire-
shovel-like stirrups, and bridle-bits heavily gilt.
Other members of the Embassy, both ladies and
gentlemen, received a horse or a mule each, and the
gentlemen a finely ornamented sword. My wife,

whose popularity amongst the ladies of Sid Moosa's harem had perhaps something to do with the matter, was presented, besides a nice little Barb horse, with some finely embroidered articles, which were duly appreciated. For myself, I was consoled with a handsome silver-mounted sword, with gold-embroidered belt. The quantity of cotton cloths, haics, belts, and slippers distributed amongst the servants would have made the fortunes of a dozen shopkeepers in the bazaar.

The Sultan of Morocco never moves without an army at his heels. The plain to the south of the city was covered with the conical tents of a host that could not have numbered less than ten thousand men. We often passed through them, and were invariably treated with respect. It was pleasant to see the groups of swarthy men cooking, playing draughts, or otherwise amusing themselves. In their midst was the Sultan's tent, distinguished only by its greater size and by a canvas wall that ran round it so as to form a circular courtyard.

One Friday, when the Sultan went to the mosque and reviewed his troops, I witnessed their return to camp through the palace gate. Each regiment was preceded by its officers to the number of seven or eight; then came hatchet-armed pioneers, then drummers and buglers all in full thrum and blast. Next the rank-and-file in rows of three, four, five, six, seven, or eight deep, apparently according to their own sweet will. The marching was what might be expected from such an arrangement. As to size, age, and other respects, our volunteer regiments present uniformity itself in comparison. Some were stooping greybeards, others boys of fourteen or fifteen years of age, some pure negroes, many half-breeds, but the majority were pure Arabs. The dress was a red flannel jacket and waistcoat with blue cotton trousers or rather breeches, for the legs were bare from the knee. Here and there blue-coated men might be seen, and the regimental flags were in some cases red, and in others quarantine yellow. All the men wore slippers down at the heels, to walk in which, an art in itself, is by no means conducive to the regularity of a "march past." They were armed with old flint and percussion muskets intermixed. The kaids or colonels were the only mounted men. Whether from love or fear, probably the latter, the officers were held in due respect. One of my guards rushed at his kaid as he rode slowly past, and kissed his knees in a very affectionate manner.

After the long procession of regulars (?) had passed, there issued forth a mob of mounted white-robed cavalry, the Bashi-Bazouks of the Moorish army.

But so far as concerns military discipline, after many previous failures, the Moorish Government

seem resolved on adopting the tactics of Europe
in good earnest. A few of their soldiers were
being trained in the garrison of Gibraltar, and
Lieutenant Maclean, a young officer of great
promise in the English service, had recently been
appointed instructor-in-chief with the title of
kaid. At Tangier I had the pleasure of accompanying him on the occasion of his first drill.
As this was necessarily conducted through an
interpreter, it was particularly hard work. But
intelligence and good physique, the two main
factors in the formation of troops, were plainly
marked in the disorderly mob of fifty or sixty
men who turned out. It was comical to see the
anxiety of the officers to make a good appearance
for the nonce as the men took ground for their
new experience. An idea of the rudimentary
state of the Moorish tactics may be obtained
when it is stated that the simple formation in
fours was unknown in the Moorish army.

CHAPTER III.

IT will be remembered that our destination was
in the first instance Fez, until obliged to follow the
movements of the Sultan to Mequinez. Sixteen
days' residence in the latter place had exhausted all
the sights, and His Majesty expressed a wish that
we should visit his northern capital. The Spanish
proverb says, " See Seville and die." In the eyes
of the Moors, Fez seems to take the place of Seville :
Mequinez was held to be perfect in its way, but
everything was to be seen, everything on earth was
to be had at Fez ; and to Fez we accordingly
directed our course.

We left Mequinez by its northern gate, outside
which were some fine perennial springs, at which
men were perpetually engaged in washing clothes,
or else themselves or their horses. The rising

ground beyond this commanded a view of the town
which was really grand. Then came olive planta-
tions of great extent, enclosed by a long wall at
about two miles distance from the town. Ten miles
farther on we came to a small river, the Wad Jedida.
It was spanned by a substantial bridge of brick and
stone with a platform like a piece of a towing
path beneath the arch at each side. Our breakfast
was spread on one of these, so that we had perfect
shelter from the sun's rays. It was a lovely
spot. Oleanders and other luxuriant shrubs fringed
the banks, and vines clustered round them;
where the ground was drier, the beautiful flowers
of the caper plant bloomed profusely. The river
was full of a kind of perch, which amused us
greatly by the scramble which every bit of bread
thrown to them produced. Here we lingered, but
once on the move, did not stop until we had
reached the Wad Enga, close to which our tents
were pitched.

We entered Fez on the following morning,
June 24th. The distance, according to my com-
putation from Mequinez, was thirty-four miles.
This time there was no public recognition of the
Embassy, but the Basha and some of the notables
of the town accompanied us.

A garden affords the most primitive, as well as
the most ancient, idea of a resting place. In the
Moorish mind the idea of its appropriateness still
prevails. Where in Europe guests would be intro-

duced to a drawing-room, in Morocco they are taken
to a garden. We were at once conducted to the
Sultan's garden, situated between Old and New Fez.
Here we rested in a shaded arbour.

As far as concerned luxuriant verdure, irrigation,
the gift of the adjoining river, made the place a
paradise. The orange groves were magnificent, but
what struck us in particular was a row of myrtles
in full bloom, having trunks like forest trees, fully
forty feet in height. The jessamines were also
gigantic. The palace buildings adjoined this
enclosure, and in a shed opening into the garden
were a couple of the quaintest looking carriages
ever seen. One was a kind of two-wheeled
brougham; both were painted and decorated in a
curious manner. Most likely they were presents
brought by some former embassy, and had never
once been used. They were now mere dilapidated
wrecks.

As it was resolved that we should not take up
quarters in the city, we encamped on the bank of a
branch of the Sebou, about half a mile from the
city wall.

The city appeared to be about two miles and a
half in length, but narrow. It was surrounded by
hills, those on the south side being so close that the
place was overlooked by them. From this eleva-
tion, with its mosques, minarets, countless houses,
and towering palms, the view was really imposing
—imposing in more than the æsthetic sense, for

distance, beyond any question in Morocco, lends enchantment. The town was divided by the river into Old and New Fez, the former being by far the most extensive, and the seat of the great industries of the place. We rode through a very long street, but only about seven feet wide, running east and west through the whole of Old Fez, the Oxford Street of the place. It was paved in some parts with stones the size and shape of cocoa-nuts, and actually polished by constant traffic. In some spots there were steep hills, and here the smoothness of the stones made it exceedingly difficult even for mules to travel. The famous Karubin, the largest mosque in Morocco, was placed on one side of this street. It was an immense building, and by peeps into its several doors we could see its endless array of pillars, and get some idea of the vast but perfectly plain interior. The shops were the usual square cells, raised some feet from the ground, open entirely in front, but larger than in other towns. They were well stocked with all kinds of merchandise.

The Moorish shopkeeper, who sits precisely in the same way as the Turkish, with all his wares within easy reach, is a less dignified personage, being more astute and eager to make sales. The Fez trader is, however, polite enough, and will ask you to take coffee, always obtainable from a neighbouring stall, to induce you to stay and bargain for his goods.

In some places, there were groups of shops in which the sellers were also the makers of their several wares. Such were the gunmakers, silversmiths, embroiderers in gold on cloth and leather, &c. We found that these men possessed little or no stock-in-trade. Everything was made to order, so that it was more difficult to obtain specimens of Moorish art than we were led to believe. The pottery, for which the place is famous, is coarse in texture and cheap in price, but really effective in the blending and arrangement of colour and variety of shape.

Many of the streets were covered with an open roof of interlaced reeds, over which vines spread in great luxuriance. These roofs, and any projections from the houses, were festooned with cobwebs, while the footway below was covered with dust and dirt. The Funduks or warehouses of the wholesale merchants had usually galleries surrounding their small square enclosures, the balustrades being unpainted and broken. Everything was shabby and mean, judged by the European standard. But what astonished us most of all was the extreme narrowness of the streets in which the private houses were situated. In some instances it would not be possible for two men to walk side by side. Nothing more dismal or cheerless could be imagined than such narrow chasms between high windowless walls. And yet these were the avenues by means of which the opulent citizens gained access, through little doors, to courtyards with marble fountains, and in their way well-appointed houses.

Fez is computed to contain about 50,000 inhabitants, and the wealth of the place is considerable. Its chief industries consist in weaving, tanning, and potteries; the red cap, for the production of which it is famous, is universally known by the name of the place itself.

The stifling heat, increased by the crowd which always followed us, made shopping in Fez irksome work. But we were treated always with courtesy and respect.

The condition of the Jews here is as bad as in other places in the interior of Morocco, and yet here, as elsewhere, some Hebrews contrive not only to live but to grow rich.

The pallor of the citizens of Fez, compared with the bronzed faces of the country Moors, is striking. It is an earthy or dirty-white paleness, which gives them a sickly look, and is without doubt due to etiolation. They rarely go outside the city walls, and inside, the sun, owing to the narrowness of the streets, hardly ever reaches them. But notwithstanding this, it does not seem to be an unhealthy community. The dryness of the climate prevents many of the bad effects of decomposition, while there is no lack of water to clear away the sewage. Every house of any pretensions has its own fountain, and public conduits and drinking fountains are numerous. The water disagrees remarkably with strangers, and the Spanish and German Embassies which preceded us suffered greatly. At my suggestion, water for our use was brought from a distance, and we escaped.

It is said that Fez contains collections of books and manuscripts in the precincts of some of the mosques, the relics of days prior to the decadence of Moorish power and intelligence. And it has been supposed that amongst these neglected records may lie some precious remains of antiquity, such as the wanting Books of Livy. Perhaps the place affords the last chance of recovering such literary treasures. Every other part of the world that might contain them has probably been already searched. I therefore set before myself the task of obtaining access to these libraries. But, notwithstanding that I was personally promised by Sid Abdalla Ben Hamed, the Governor of Fez, then in attendance on the Sultan at Mequinez, that he would write to his son, the Acting-Governor of Fez, telling him to give me access to the collections, and that the application was backed by a letter from the Sharif of Wazzan, all efforts were in vain. It seemed to be one of the many points upon which the Moors have resolved either not to gratify the curiosity or to submit to the interference of Europeans. Excuses, subterfuges, evasions, in all of which the Moor is *facile princeps*, were brought into play, and I never saw book or manuscript.

About two miles from Fez was the extensive palace called Lallah Amina, a favourite residence of the Sultan. It was placed in the midst of a very large garden, and there was an open space for the exercise of troops. We were shown a yard enclosed within high walls—one hundred paces long by fifty wide—admirably paved throughout with coloured tiles arranged in patterns. At each end was a windowless apartment, faced by a colonnade, corresponding in length with the width of the yard. There is a Spartan simplicity about all Moorish palaces. This particular one is said to have been built in the good old piratical times by captives, the majority of whom were Englishmen.

But if the old days of foreign slavery are gone for ever, there was no lack of the domestic element, which was maintained with rigour. A great addition was being made to the palace enclosure at New Fez close to our camp. The walls were constructed of *tapia*—consisting of a mixture of clay and lime, put into a casing made of parallel boards, and rammed well into a compact mass, after the method of our own south-coast builders. As the work progressed, the boards were raised and the process repeated. Gangs of black slaves were incessantly employed from daybreak to four o'clock in the afternoon at this labour. That they were kept closely at work was made evident by the perpetual song or wail

which the wretches uttered while the heavy
rammers were all raised and brought down together.   There was a cart drawn tandem by mules
in attendance upon this work, the only wheeled
vehicle, except the Sultan's coach, we had seen
in the country.

Three days sufficed for our visit to Fez, and
we left by a route to the east of that commonly
travelled, as affording a better road when the
weather is dry.   For a short distance it consisted of a broad avenue bordered with aloes.
Farther on we came upon one of those surprises
here and there met with in Morocco.   It was a
small lake, apparently frozen and snow-covered,
under a burning sun.   What seemed to be snow
was salt, left after evaporation of the water,
in which it was held in solution.   The whole
route to Woled Jemah, where we stopped, was
a succession of hills, the soil in the latter part
of it being very thin and chalky, and here caper
bushes in splendid flower grew in profusion.

As our object was now dispatch, we made
afternoon as well as morning journeys.   Two
hours from Woled Jemah brought us to a ford
of the Sebou, where it was about one hundred and
fifty yards across.   Here an amusing incident
occurred.   Senhora Colaço's Spanish maid, Dolores
by name, was no horsewoman.   Not being able
to ride in the ordinary way, she made the journey
seated in a kind of saddle chair used in Portugal.

Dolores expressed great horror at the prospect of having to cross the wide expanse of water which the river presented. But between crossing and being left behind there was no choice. Arrived at mid-stream, however, all the maiden's courage deserted her, and with one wild shriek she fell or threw herself into the water. Whether the episode was more tragic or comic, it would be hard to say. Any one might suppose that the last moments of the poor maiden had arrived, an opinion, without any doubt, held by herself. No threats and no entreaties could induce her to remount. The situation reminded one strongly of primitive baptism by immersion. The swarthy, grinning Moor that led her by the hand grotesquely represented an early father of the Church, while she might be supposed to be possessed of any number of devils strongly objecting through her mouthpiece to the sacred ceremony. Immersed to the waist for the greater part of the journey, and protesting with all her might that once back to Tangier her acquaintance with the interior of Morocco had for ever ceased, the opposite bank was at last reached.

Two journeys made the next day over hill and plain, in the course of which the wide river Wurga was forded, brought us to Hadcour.

It was a real relief to get on without let or hindrance on the score of ceremony or powder-play.

We breakfasted on the following day on the bank of a stream beautifully shaded by orange and fig trees. The surface of the water was broken now and then by tortoises popping up their heads to breathe. These unsavoury creatures—for they emit a nauseous odour—had a keen eye, or perhaps nose, for what was going on. Several big lumbering fellows soon crawled on to the bank, and seized greedily upon any fragments of meat or bread they could lay hold upon. It was a case of voracity *versus* timidity, in which the first prevailed.

That evening we reached our old encampment at Alcassar.

After leaving Alcassar, and having crossed the Lucos, our course lay westward through a country studded with cork oak trees. Here, in a small stream, some nearly naked boys were engaged in eel-fishing after a novel fashion. They were armed with knobbed sticks, with the small ends of which they poked the banks to start their game, and then clubbed them dexterously with the heavy ends.

On nearing the town of Larache, we were met by the Governor with a guard of askars, and a band of drums and bugles. As we passed, the soldiers presented arms after a manner, and the band, greatly to our astonishment, struck up the Rogue's March! The Moors are not adepts in European music, and the selection in the present case in honour of the Ambassador and his suite could hardly be considered happy.

El Araish, corrupted by Europeans into Larache, is picturesquely situated at the mouth of the river Lucos, itself a corruption for El Kus. A treacherous bar, marked by the remains of vessels projecting out of the sandbanks, prevents the port from being much frequented. These remains gave the place a melancholy aspect. The mind pictured to itself a vessel like a thing of life rushing to unseen destruction. And the denuded timbers recalled the ghastly spectacle of some skeleton with its fleshless ribs of camel or horse, or even of man himself, as one has seen them on some lonely desert.

Larache is built on a steep hill rising from the sea. Like all Moorish towns, it is surrounded by a high wall with battlements. The streets are fairly wide, and this, as well as some existing buildings, are due to a previous occupation by the Portuguese. The population is about 4,000, one-sixth of which are Jews, and there are sixty-seven Europeans, all told. To Mr. L. Ford, the one solitary English resident, we were indebted for much attention.

We crossed the river in a boat with fourteen rowers, reminding one of the galleys of former days. Our route now lay over sand hills, and then over hills covered with myrtles and other shrubs in full bloom. At length the route by which we came was struck at Resana, and later on Garbia was reached.

Our Moors were here highly entertained by a professional shooter of the William Tell school, who came into camp. This man had a companion, who fixed an onion by its stalk on the top of his head so that it stood clear of it by a couple of inches. The game was to shoot the onion off the man's head without killing him. The marksman stood, or sat, or lay down at a distance of about five yards from the onion, and hit the mark once in three or four times amid the applause of the spectators. The gun used was the ordinary unwieldy Moorish weapon, and leaden bolts were extemporaneously beaten out to fit it by means of a hammer and small anvil carried for the purpose.

During this home journey, the sun's rays late and early were almost overpowering to animals as well as to men. The horses suffered much, and we noticed that sheep which we passed adopted a curious mode of sheltering themselves. They stood in groups, one having its head under the stomach of the other.

However, we reached Tangier safely on July 2nd, the sixth day from leaving Fez, and exactly six weeks from our departure.

I may be allowed, in conclusion, to express our

obligations to Senhor and Senhora Colaço for much courtesy and kindness, and to the other members of the party for many attentions which tended to make the journey pleasant. The gracious acts, and the uniform politeness, of the Moorish authorities, are also gratefully acknowledged.

APPENDIX A.

THREE centuries ago, on August 4th, 1578, the tragedy known in Portuguese history as the battle of Alcassar el Kebir took place. A short account of it may interest the reader.*

To possess himself of the whole empire of Morocco, where he already held Tangier and other towns on the coast, was the great ambition of Don Sebastian, the young king. The monarchy was at the time badly prepared for such a strain on its resources as a Moorish war, on account of the recent conquests and settlements in India. Troops were, however, sought after in all possible quarters. A small contingent of six or seven hundred Pontifical soldiers was obtained in so strange a way as to be worth special notice.

Thomas Stukeley, an Englishman, said to have been created Marquis of Leinster by the Pope, sailed from Civita Vecchia as commander of this force. It was destined to aid a rebellion in Ireland, and the Genoese vessel in which it was embarked put into Lisbon at the

* This account is mainly taken from a very interesting work, "Les Faux Don Sebastien," par Miguel D'Antas. Paris, 1866. The distinguished author is the present representative of Portugal at the British Court.

moment when the king was in the midst of his warlike preparations. He contrived to excite the hopes of the soldiers and of their commander so effectually that they abandoned the design upon which they were despatched, and took service against the heretic Moors instead of against the heretic Queen Elizabeth.

Muley Ahmed Ben Abdallah, the Sultan's brother and claimant of his throne, who was at Tangier, constantly urged that an army should be sent to Africa, and that success was certain. But he counselled that the king should not accompany it, lest the party opposed to the Sultan might suspect that the conquest and occupation of the whole country was contemplated.

At length, on July 6th, the Portuguese forces reached Tangier, and, after a short delay, proceeded to Arzila. The Sultan Abd-el-Melek now made peaceful overtures to the king, which were rejected with disdain.

On July 29th the army left Arzila, and, after some marching and counter-marching, proceeded along the right bank of the M'Hassen river. The object in view was to capture the town of Alcassar. On the night of August 3rd, the army had on its left the M'Hassen, and on its right another tributary of the Lucos. But the provisions of this ill-starred expedition were already falling short, and it was decided to cross the M'Hassen at once. A bridge, which still exists, was used for crossing, and as the engagement began immediately after, it is sometimes called the Battle of the Bridge. Men and officers were confident of success, and the young king, urged by his courtiers, longed for the fray. One of them, it is recorded, jocosely begged that, after the coming victory, the Sultan's ears, which he said he would eat with oil and vinegar, should be allotted to him.

The Portuguese army is stated to have numbered about 15,000 infantry, chiefly pikemen, and 2,400 cavalry, with thirty-six pieces of artillery. The Moorish host is said to have numbered 40,000 cavalry with 14,000 or 15,000 infantry, accompanied by forty cannon. His Moorish ally counselled Sebastian not to provoke a battle until the sun's rays were declining, urging that the Moors could so much better than the Europeans endure the mid-day heat. But no warning availed with the doomed monarch.

In the great plain which extends from the M'Hassen to Alcassar, the ground is in one place slightly elevated. It is said that the Sultan's infantry and artillery drawn up here were carefully screened from view by a vast quantity of boughs of trees conveyed to the spot, so artfully arranged as to resemble a natural thicket. Behind the hill the main body of the cavalry was posted, while on each of its sides 10,000 mounted Arabs were arranged as supports to the concealed centre of the host. The gallant Portuguese army, led by the fiery young king, always, and at this moment more than ever, jealous of the supreme command, rushed into the jaws of this deadly ambuscade. It was not until they arrived almost at the foot of the hill, and when the Moorish cannon all at once thundered upon them, that the mistake was discovered. Discharge after discharge from the enemies' guns threw the Christians, who, in the midst of their confusion, halted for a brief prayer, into terrible disorder. The Portuguese attack was partial, a large portion of the army having remained inactive, a mishap caused, it is said, by the folly of the king, who directed that no movement should be made except by his express orders.

Now ensued a deadly encounter signalized by such feats of arms as might be expected from valorous troops, and the cavalry of the Duke d'Aveiro particularly distinguished themselves. A portion of the army penetrated the Moorish host, so far that its commander, in an evil moment, checked the advance. This was the turning-point of the day. The Portuguese were now so closely surrounded on all sides, that they had hardly space to use their arms. Every attempt was made to save the king, who, when he could have retreated, refused. Forgetting that the part of the commander was not that of the actual combatant, he headed more than one desperate charge in which, while inflicting losses on the enemy, his own followers fell in numbers. As a last effort a flag of truce was displayed, and the Portuguese and Moorish officers agreed to respect the royal person. But when asked to give up his sword, Sebastian shouted in reply, "A king should lose his liberty only with his life." While at the same instant, followed by a few of his noble guards, he dashed into the midst of his enemies. From that time he was never again seen alive.

It was the death of this prince which caused such calamities, owing to a disputed succession, to the realm of Portugal, and led to its union with Spain for sixty years afterwards. And it was the sad yet chivalrous ending of his career, together with the uncertainty about his exact fate in a barbarous land, that caused the young king to be at last regarded as a supernatural personage. Year after year his return from Africa was looked for, and even when centuries had rolled by, the reappearance of Sebastian was not regarded as an impossibility by the populace of Portugal.

APPENDIX B.*

THE SITE OF THE ROMAN CITY OF VOLUBILIS.

THE identification of an ancient city is always a matter of great interest, and with this object in view I carefully examined the remarkable ruins called Cassar Pharaon (Pharaoh's Castle), situated about twelve miles north-east from Mequinez, and about twenty-eight miles north-west from Fez. The ruins lie out of the direct road to either of these places; but the fact that they have been so seldom visited by Europeans is due not so much to this circumstance as to the extreme jealousy with which the adjacent Zaouia or sanctuary of Muley Edris is guarded.

Rohlfs, who travelled as a Mussulman, and was thus able to enter the sanctuary, makes no mention of the ruins. He says, in connection with his visit, that he was "always looked upon with distrust—to ask directly about any place would not do at all, I should have been at once denounced as a spy."† Following Leo Africanus, he supposes the town of Muley Edris to occupy the site of Volubilis. I shall have more to say on this subject hereafter.

This Muley Edris was the father of him of the same name by whom the city of Fez was founded. The town in connection with the sanctuary is placed on the southern declivities of two cone-shaped elevations of a mountain called Zarhoun. The ruins are situated at a distance of about two miles from the town upon a level platform, in part supported by a wall, beyond which the ground slopes abruptly towards the south. To the west of the ruins, blocks of hewn stone are scattered over a considerable space, with here and there Roman carved work in scrolls, and egg and tongue patterns, &c. All

* This description appeared in the *Academy* of June 29, 1878.

† "Adventures in Morocco," pp. 120, 199. By Dr. Gerhard Rohlfs. (London, 1874.)

these stones, as well as those of the standing portions of the buildings and of the tombs, are of the same material —namely, grey limestone.

The ruins appear to belong to the late Roman period. One of them consists of the remains of a building which measured externally thirty-six yards in length by twenty yards in breadth. Two large archways still exist in the portions of the walls that formed the ends of the structure, as seen in the reproduction of a photograph

taken by myself. The southern wall, of which most remains, is about forty feet in height. It is interesting to find that Windus—who visited the place 156 years previously, under the same circumstances, having accompanied an embassy—gives a drawing and a short description of the ruins.* He describes the ruin now

* "A Journey to Mequinez, &c.; on the Occasion of Commodore Stewart's Embassy thither for the Redemption of the British Captives in the year 1721" (London, 1725), p. 85.

under consideration as the " good part of the front of a large square building . . . . parts of the four corners are yet standing, but very little remains, except these, of the front." Since Windus wrote, the whole of the front and the corresponding wall at the back have entirely disappeared, except so much of them as is almost on a level with the ground. No cement appears to have been used, and the stones in the standing walls in some places show spaces of an inch or two in the perpendicular join-

ings. In other cases, the blocks are in such positions as to threaten to fall out of the edges of the walls. It is plain that these effects could only have been produced by a rocking movement in definite directions. It is almost certain, therefore, that a succession of earthquake shocks acting in the direction of north and south have prostrated the front wall described by Windus, and at the same time shaken the stones of the end walls loose in the manner above described.

At a distance of 100 yards towards the north on the

same platform, and facing in the same direction, but at a slightly diverging angle, stand the remains of an arch. The archway was twenty feet wide, and from the massiveness of the structure (as shown in the above view, also from a photograph taken by me), and from the circumstance that its back and front were alike, it was probably a triumphal arch. This was the opinion of Windus, whose drawing of it represents the arch as unbroken. Underneath it, he found six fragments of stones that contained portions of inscriptions (also figured by him), which he says, "were fixed higher [on the arch] than any part now standing." A portion of one of these fragments was identified by me. The remainder probably lie buried in the *débris* of the fallen arch.* A mutilated bust in bas-relief, figured by Windus, is also still to be seen. Many pieces of pilasters, pillars, and Corinthian capitals are strewn about the platform. Besides fragments of buildings, the abrupt slope previously men-

* The fragment I saw contained slender-shaped letters about six inches in length. All the portions of inscriptions figured by Windus were too fragmentary for anything to be made out of them, and he made no attempt of the kind. Sebaste, the Greek rendering of Augustus, appeared on one of them, and the repetition of the letters M Λ X indicated that the inscriptions were connected with something imperial, probably the record of a triumph. Windus says of the ruins: "Which the Moors call Cassar Pharaon (*i.e.* Pharaoh's Castle), who they told us was a Christian, but could not give any further account thereof. A draught of which, with the Inscriptions of several stones found in the ruins, I have taken, for the consideration of the curious." I have found another view of the ruins, in the same state as when drawn by Windus, in a work entitled "Several Voyages to Barbary" (2nd ed., London, 1736, p. 141). The only reference to the plate is contained in the following passage. Speaking of slaves at Mequinez, it is stated:—"One of them, Capt. Henry Boyd (since deceased), having taken a plan of that place, with some sketch of the slaves' employment there, we thought fit to insert it, together with three other draughts of his, viz., a coast chart, some Roman ruins, and a plan of Alcasar, which possibly may be acceptable to the curious, tho' not immediately relating to the present subject."

tioned has upon it several tombs apparently still intact. Two of these bear inscriptions of which Windus makes no mention. The larger one is covered by a slab almost on a level with the soil. Before describing this, I have to make a few observations.

It was a curious coincidence that the inscription on this slab, copied into a German journal, reached the *Academy* at the same time (August 4th) that a letter of mine, stating that I was about to make a communication about Volubilis and its inscriptions, was already in type for insertion in that journal. Circumstances prove that the long-neglected inscription in question was copied independently within a very few days by members of the German Embassy to the Sultan and by myself, assisted by the Portuguese Ambassador and Mr. C. Murdoch.

The thick slab in question is about five feet long by three feet wide, and is badly fractured longitudinally. The inscription is contained within a border of scroll-work ornament. Here is an exact copy of that made with much care by myself. The lines are numbered for convenience of reference :—

1. QCAECILIOQFILIO
2. DOMITIANOCLVDIA
3. VOLVBILIIANODICV
4. RIONIMUNICIPII
5. VOLVBILIIANIAN
6. NORVMX QCAE
7. CIIIVSS   ACRA
8. CIIISIICM
9. ANTONIANI
10. IISIIIIOIII
11.   IOS

Note, in lines 7, 8, and 10, the repetition of the letter I occurs because what is chiefly apparent in most cases is that the letters possessed upright lines. It is easy, however, in the majority of the cases to make out the letters to which these lines undoubtedly belonged. The reading of this by Prof. Mommsen, as given in the *Academy* August 4th, is :—

"Q(uinto) Cæcilio Q(uinti) filio Domitiano Claudia Volubiliano, decurioni municipii Volubiliani, annorum XX, Q(uintus) Cæcilius . . . . . (et) Antonia N(ata)lis filio pii(ssimo) posueru(nt)."

This agrees with my reading and interpretation, with the following exceptions. It is, however, to be observed that the exact copy of the inscription sent to this eminent authority is not before us.

Line 3. A letter is omitted: it is "Volubiliiano," or "Volubilliano," not "Volubiliano."

Line 5. The same omission occurs.

Line 6. I could not decipher the letter which succeeded X, owing to the fracture of the stone. The hiatus is filled in the German copy by a second X.

Line 7. In my copy after "Caecilius," S occurs, and with a hiatus of two or three letters, owing to the increased damage from the fracture; the letters "acra" are quite readable. This portion of the inscription is not included in the reading by Mommsen given above. But he says: "I cannot decipher the cognomen and position of the father; perhaps there stood something like 'Gracilis leg[ionis] I.'" Evidently these words were conjectured by reading the antepenultimate letter of line 7 as G, and making up the remainder from the letters and portions of letters in line 8, except the last letter; this is plainly M.

Line 9. Both copies agree with the exception of the last letter, which I make I, and Prof. Mommsen conjecturally A.

Line 10. The letters are very imperfect, but from their arrangement and general appearance, and comparison with other inscriptions, no doubt can be entertained that the words "Filio piissimo" were inscribed.

Line 11. The same remarks apply to IOS, which is certainly to be read "posuerunt."

The circumstance that the monument is in memory of a native of Volubilis, and one of its municipal officers, affords strong presumptive evidence that it was placed at Volubilis.

The other monumental inscription is on the perpendicular face of a block of stone about two feet square. There are two holes in the top of the stone, which seem to have been intended for attaching something to it, possibly a statue. The inscription is as follows :—

```
M F Λ B I O L I I L C I
R O G Λ T O Λ N X V I I
L E Λ B I V S C R I S P V S
P Λ T E R
F I L I O P I I S S I M O
P O S
```

"M(arco) Fabio . . . . Rogato An(norum) XVII Leabius (*sic*) Crispus Pater Filio piissimo pos(uit)."

That Volubilis was an important place may be judged from the ruins described—assuming, as I believe, that they belonged to that city—and from the mention of it by many ancient authors. Pliny says:[*]

"Ab Lixo XL. M. in Mediterraneo altera Augusti colonia est Babba, Julia Campestris appellata; et tertia Banasa, LXXV. M., Valentia cognominata. Ab ea XXXV. M. pass. Volubilis oppidum tantundem a mari utroque distans."

There can be no doubt that the Lixus river of Pliny is identical with the modern El Kus or Lucos river. But as the positions of Babba and Banasa are open to doubt, the distances given here can help us little in fixing the position of Volubilis. But the distance of the sanctuary of Muley Edris from either sea—that is, from the Mediterranean and the Atlantic—as shown on the best map of Morocco,[†] accords well with Pliny's statement. The map shows that Volubilis was somewhat nearer to the Atlantic

[*] "Natural History," B. v. c. 1.

[†] "Carte de l'Empire de Maroc. Reduite et gravée au Dépôt Général de la Guerre." (Paris, 1848.)

than to the Mediterranean, if we place it close to Muley
Edris. But if it be assigned to the site of the modern
city of Fez it would be considerably nearer to the Mediterranean than to the Atlantic. Ptolemy mentions Οὐολου-
βιλίς in his tables of the positions of places,[*] but it is
impossible in this case also to fix that of this city by his
aid.

In one edition of Pomponius Mela, Volubilis is mentioned as one of the principal cities of Mauretania
Tingitana;[†] in another edition the word Dubritania is
substituted.[‡]

The question arises whether the site of Volubilis was
not that of the modern city of Fez as alleged by some
authors. If the distances given in the *Itinerarium
Antonini* could be trusted, Fez must be adopted as the
site. He states that Volubilis was "*Mill. pass.* xvi." from
Aquae Dacicae.[§] Hot springs were known to have
existed here, and at about the distance mentioned from
Fez is the hot sulphurous water of Ain Sidi Yussuf, which
is unquestionably identical with Aquae Dacicae. But
from the many known errors with regard to distances in
this author, it would be rash to accept his statement as a
proof.

Hemso says :—

"Volubilis, o Volobilis, da molti creduta Fas, ma piu precisamente
la Tiulit, e Gualili dei secoli di mezzo, e la Zauiat Mula-Driss dei
nostri giorni."[§]

In all that concerns Morocco, no author is so much quoted
as Leo, who wrote in the sixteenth century; and his
statements may in general be relied on. He asserts that
the town which contained the sepulchre of Muley Edris
on Mount Zarhoun, was called Gualili, and was built by

---

[*] "Geography," Book iv. c. 1.

[†] "Chorographia." Edit. Vossii (Frankerae, 1700).

[‡] "Chorographia." Edit. Gustav Parthey (Berolini, 1867).

[§] "Specchio geografico e statistico dell' imperio di Marocco, del-
cavliere conte Jacopo Graberg di Hemso" (Geneva, 1834).

the Romans. Some author, struck perhaps by the possible transmutation of Volubilis (not mentioned by Leo) into Gualili, concluded that the modern town had succeeded to the ancient one. This statement has been often repeated without question. But a reference to Leo's work* will show that he also speaks " of a certaine towne called the Palace of Pharao," as being also founded by the Romans, and about eight miles from Gualili. The distance here given, even supposing the miles to be of the shortest description, makes it improbable that Leo visited the place. After combating the idea that the town was built by Pharaoh, King of Egypt, he says : " I am rather of opinion, by the Latine letters which are engraven on the walles, that the Romans built this towne."

My inquiries lead me to believe that the name Gualili is not known in connection with Muley Edris at the present time. And while I think it highly improbable that an important city like Volubilis would be placed on the steep declivity of a mountain, it seems to me reasonable to suppose that from the proximity of the two places the now obsolete name Gualili, assuming it to be derived from Volubilis, would easily be transferred by mistake or otherwise from one place to the other.

The position of the ruins is one admirably adapted for an important city. It commands a fine view over an extensive and fertile plain. It is central as regards the northern portion of Morocco, and on the direct road to many of the remoter parts. The ruins and inscriptions are of particular interest, because they are the most westerly remains of the far-extending Roman Empire.

* "A Geographical Historie of Africa," by John Leo a More. Translated by John Pory (London, 1600).

APPENDIX C.

I VENTURED to test the influence I had gained at the
Moorish court by my connection with the embassy as well
as by the turn of events by asking certain favours. I
was aware that the high officials were by no means con-
ciliatory to strangers, and that a gentleman who had
approached the chief minister a short time previously
with an introduction from the best possible quarter was
not even granted an audience. I asked Sid Moosa to
obtain from the Sultan a document which should act
as a safe conduct for a journey to Timbuctoo, or at all
events as far as the Sultan's power extended. Not that
I had formed a definite plan for so perilous a journey,
but it seemed to me that as the greater includes the less,
I might obtain a passport of great value for a future
journey in the remoter parts of Morocco. Contrary to
the opinion of my friends, which was that the Moorish
Government would not issue a document which might be
a cause of embarrassment to them, the request was received
favourably. Sid Moosa had a paper drawn up, which
though short is of great power. Here is its *fac simile*.

اُذنّا لحاملِهِ الطبيبِ الانگليزيِّ اَنجنُكارِهِ اِياالتنا الْمحرُوسة بِاللهِ وَلا فَتخَـار
عَلَ انخابِ الّتِي تَنَالُهَا لاحُكُكم مِنْ نَجْ اَن يورِطَ نَفسَهُ مَ الْمَواضِع الَّنَّ تَنَالُها
لاحُكّام قَنـامُرتَنزيَكَهَا عَليْنَ مِنْ حُكّامِنَا وَقبَا بِلِهَا عَنِنَا المُطِيعِيـنَ
اَنيُقابِلُهُ بِالجَمِيل وِاَنَ لُهُ اِمكَانَا حَتّى يَطِلهُ مَنّ وَ مِنْ اَحَد وَالكلاَ
٢١ جمادَ نَطَ ١٢٩٤

"Praise to the One God.

"There is no strength nor power but in God Almighty the Most High.

"We have granted permission to the bearer, the English Doctor, to travel in our Dominions protected by God, and to visit the tribes who are under the control of the Government, but he is not to expose (his life) in parts where they are not under control. We order our governors and obedient tribes to take care of him, and give him assistance, and to receive him with kindness and attention, so that no injury may befall him from any one.

"Peace,

"12 Jumad the Second, 1294.
(25th June, 1877.)"

It is in the seal, which is that of the Sultan himself, that the virtue of this edict resides. If handed to one of his subjects, it is first reverently applied to his forehead and then kissed devoutly. Such a passport, bearing the ministerial seal, is now and then issued, but one bearing the Imperial talisman does not appear to have been given to any previous traveller. As if to show still more good faith in the matter, the paper was forwarded through the hands of His Excellency Sir John Drummond Hay, at Tangier, whose popularity with the Moorish Government is very great. It was accompanied by a letter to him from Sid Moosa, pointing out the danger of an attempt to reach Timbuctoo. The fate that befel my application to examine the libraries at Fez has been elsewhere detailed.

APPENDIX D.

ITINERARY of journey from Tangier to Mequinez and Fez. The distances were estimated from the walking pace of a mule, namely four miles an hour. Stoppages even of five minutes were always deducted. The temperature of the atmosphere in the shade is also given:—

Date.	Time occupied in travelling.	Miles.	Temperature in the shade.			Names of Stopping Places and Remarks.
			Early morning.	Mid-day.	At night.	
May	h. min		Fah.	Fah.	Fah.	
21	3·30	14			74	{ Left Tangier; camped at Kaa el Urmil.
22	3	12	69	83	71	Garbia.
23	5·40	22⅔	70	86	72	Klatta de Raissana.
24	4	16	72	91	73	Alcassar.
25	4·20	17⅓	69	90	70	Ben Ouda.
26	2·35	10⅓	71	90	72	Habassie.
27	2·40	10⅔	69	88	73	Beni Hassan.

JOURNEY FROM TANGIER—*continued.*

Date.	Time occupied in travelling.	Miles.	Temperature in the shade.			Names of Stopping Places and Remarks.
			Early morning.	Mid-day.	At night	
May	h.min		Fah.	Fah.	Fah.	
28	4·45	19	70	89	74	
29			72	90	71	} Bokhara.
30			74	93	77	
31	3.40	14⅔	72	91	67	
June						Zacouta.
1			74	94	80	A thunderstorm in the
2			74	99	78	evening, with some
3			74	88	68	rain.
4			68	86	72	
5	2	8	69	91	67	Cassar Pharaon.
6	1·45	7	94	102		Wad Cazar.
7	1·30	6	76	80	79	Arrived at Mequinez; total time spent in travelling, 39h. 25m.; distance, 157⅔ miles.
8			72	84		
9			82	87	84	
10			83	89	86	
11			83	85	81	
12			80	81	80	
13			79	82	79	Thunderstorm.
14			78	81	77	Mequinez.
15			78	80	79	Thunderstorm.
16			78	81	78	
17			78	82	78	
18			77	79	77	
19			77	79	77	
20			77	78	77	
21			76	77	75	
22			75	77	76	
23	5·40	22⅔	74			Left Mequinez: stopped a little beyond Wad Enga.

G

JOURNEY FROM TANGIER—*continued.*

Date.	Time occupied in travelling.	Miles.	Temperature in the shade.			Names of Stopping Places and Remarks.
			Early morning.	Mid-day.	At night.	
June	h.min		Fah.	Fah.	Fah.	Fez; time spent in travelling between Mequinez and Fez, 8h. 25m.; distance, 33⅔m.
24	2·45	11	74		74	
25			74	98		
26			72	91	77	Left Fez; camped at Hezana.
27	6·50	27⅓	69		72	Hezana.
28	8·45	35	70		74	Hadcour.
29	7	28	70		82	Alcassar.
30	5·10	20⅔	72		80	Larache.
July 1	6·55	27⅔	74		77	Garbia.
2	5·35	22⅓	75		77	Arrived at Tangier; time spent in travelling from Fez to Tangier, 40h. 15m.; distance, 161 miles.

APPENDIX E.

BEFORE leaving with the Embassy, I made an excursion with my wife to Tetuan, which was very interesting. In that part of the country there is no difficulty on the score of safety. My former guide, the redoubtable Kador, accompanied us, together with a soldier mounted on a sumpter mule.

In the early morning of May 10th, we rode out of the south gate of Tangier for some distance along the smooth sands of the bay. Then inland and over two small stone bridges across a winding river; next along its banks fringed with oleanders in full flower. The country was astir for once. Much of it was cultivated, and ploughing and maize-sowing were in active progress. Birds were in full song, and here and there the blue convolvulus was massed in large patches as effectively as if done by the most skilful cultivator. In other places were patches of mallows of bright pink and other colours. There had been rain recently, and the contrast of various flowers set in tender green charmed the eye. It is the custom with some people to decry Morocco as an arid wilderness, but this comes from the misfortune of only having seen it after or during the long summer drought. Now and then we came upon the beautiful white flowers of a bulb (*Ornithogalum arabicum*),* besides other flowers quite new to us. Plains and valleys and streams were traversed until at length the Funduk, or so-called half-way house, with its stone wall enclosure, was gained. The journey to this place, which my aneroid showed to be 700 feet above the sea level, occupied five hours and a half.

There were some fine olive trees close to a well of good water, and here we lunched, in company with a gentleman from Lima, whose taste for travelling had brought him to this out-of-the-way spot.

The road from this place lay through a mountain pass, and was extremely rough and rocky. After the lapse of an hour from starting, Tetuan was seen in the distance, but soon disappeared. When again seen, the place remained long in view, not seeming to become much nearer, in spite of our exertions to reach it. At length the stone bridge over the river that flows to Tetuan was reached, and we entered the town soon afterwards. The

* A list of plants, collected by me during this visit to Morocco, but chiefly on the journey with the Embassy, has been printed in the "Spicilegium Floræ Marocanæ," by John Ball, F.R.S. (London, 1878); a work of great industry.

last portion of the journey occupied four hours and a half, and, according to my computation, the distance between Tangier and Tetuan was exactly forty miles.

We went to the house of Isaac Nahon, an Israelite, as his named showed, and an obliging host. Here we took our ease in our inn, tired enough after the long hot ride What then was our surprise to find that a courier came in from Tangier, about an hour after our arrival, bringing me a letter of introduction from Signor Colaço for Signor Salvador Hassan, the Spanish Vice-Consul. The promised letter had been forgotten, and was most kindly forwarded after our departure from Tangier. Postal service in Morocco is substituted by a class of couriers, who, by practice, get over astonishing distances in a single day, and maintain the same pace for many days together.

Nahon's visitors' book dated from 1838, and contained the names of many distinguished persons who have made the journey from Tangier, or else came by sea.

Tetuan is situated in a verdant valley at the foot of picturesque mountains, the highest of which, called Beni Hosmar, form part of the lesser Atlas chain. The river which flows by it, and which was said to contain real troùt, was flanked with orange orchards, and dotted with the country houses of the townspeople. A swampy plain extended towards the sea, and there was a road, probably the best in all Morocco, six miles long through it to San Martin, the port. This road was made by the Spaniards during their three years' occupation of the place, and boasted, we were told, of a traffic in which two or three carts were conspicuous.

Tetuan is a much larger and more imposing place than Tangier. The streets differed little from those of other Moorish towns; but there was a large open space of between three and four acres in extent. On the north side of this was a large mosque, while the other three sides were surrounded by shops and workshops. These were almost all occupied by gunmakers, one of the chief of whom, Hadge Abdeslam el Fassy, was good enough to tell me much about his branch of industry—which was the leading one of the place. The whole number of workshops was about 100. But, contrary to what one would have expected to find, there was a division of labour; some were barrel, others lock makers, others finishers. The higher priced, gold inlaid specimens of these ungainly flint-lock weapons must be admitted to have been fairly well finished. But one could not help wondering why the Moors in this matter, as in every thing else, persistently ignore modern improvements.

A good deal of gold embroidery was done at Tetuan; and another branch of industry was the manufacture of brackets, chests, and other wood work, ornamented with arabesque painting, in brilliant colours. Slipper making and other leather work was also carried on extensively.

Signor Hassan was good enough to take us to see the houses of three rich Moors, as the best specimens which the place afforded. They had, as usual, gardens, with fine fruit trees attached to them; also terraces, fountains, and small ponds, containing gold fish, &c. The houses were different, and in some respects better than any one had seen in the interior of the country. Proximity to Europe had plainly had its effect. Some of the rooms were of large size, and besides being beautifully decorated in the Moorish style with tiled floors, in elaborate patterns, covered with rich carpets, were supported by pillars, and had glass windows. The European ornaments could not be praised; there were mirrors, artificial flowers, and clocks without end. Musical boxes also prevailed. Brackets, of Moorish design, held not only specimens of Moorish pottery, but some very good pieces of china, chiefly old Oriental. These, of course, could not be purchased. But who would have thought it? Even Morocco has been invaded by the insatiable bric-a-brac hunter.

About five years previously the then Spanish vice-consul set to work and bought up all the old china that he could, which had hitherto found a resting place here. According to Nahon's account, he made a good harvest. There was a Spanish convent at Tetuan, presided over by Padre F. Jose de Larchundi, to whom I presented a letter, and by whom I was courteously received. The success of the mission in making converts was the same as that of all missions amongst Moslems—none whatever.

Tetuan was stated to be a healthy place, in which pulmonary consumption was almost unknown. Only two or three lepers were known to be in the town.

On the third day after our arrival we left Tetuan by the road already traversed—having the rare advantage of a cloudy day for the journey—and reached Tangier safely.

PARDON AND SON, PRINTERS, PATERNOSTER ROW, LONDON.

"We learn with pleasure that so specially qualified an observer has published the results of a tour which he made in Morocco."—*Saunder's News Letter*.

"The book is full of information on all subjects that interest those who wish to improve those countries which border on civilization."—*Edinburgh Courant*.

"The appendices, contrary to general experience, are of great interest, and in that respect, as well as in their aptitude, they correspond with the contents of the volume."—*Illustrated London News*.

"Abounds in amusingly-told adventures encountered by the author during his journeys in the interior, and with valuable information."—*The Graphic*.

"He saw and heard enough to enable him to supply much valuable information."—*Pall Mall Gazette*.

"His 'plain narrative,' as he styles it, will prove both amusing to the general reader and valuable to the intending traveller."—*The Queen*.

"A very readable book, and one which to the ordinary reader may impart a good deal of knowledge and a fair amount of interest."—*Saturday Review*.

"The author has written in an agreeable and at times a picturesque style, and we very strongly recommend the book to all who desire information about a country almost unknown to the world."—*The Jewish World*.

"All the information that Dr. Leared gives as acquired from his own observation is perfectly to be relied on, and is highly interesting."—*Vanity Fair*.

"A book full of knowledge, the result of close enquiry and keen observation."—*Art Journal*.

"Altogether Dr. Leared's book is eminently readable and instructive."—*The Lancet*.

"The gatherings of a physician brought into contact with climates hardly to be excelled, if equalled, in any part of the world."—*British Medical Journal*.

"His work does him no little credit as an accomplished observer and traveller."—*Medical Times and Gazette*.

"The book is a thoroughly good and instructive one, and we have read it from cover to cover with much interest."—*The British Quarterly Review*.

LONDON: SAMPSON LOW, MARSTON, & CO.

A Catalogue of American and Foreign Books Published or Imported by MESSRS. SAMPSON LOW & CO. *can be had on application.*

Crown Buildings, 188, *Fleet Street, London, October,* 1878.

𝔄 𝔏𝔦𝔰𝔱 𝔬𝔣 𝔅𝔬𝔬𝔨𝔰

PUBLISHED BY

SAMPSON LOW, MARSTON, SEARLE, & RIVINGTON.

———◆———

ALPHABETICAL LIST.

A CLASSIFIED Educational Catalogue of Works published in Great Britain. Demy 8vo, cloth extra. Second Edition, revised and corrected to Christmas, 1877, 5*s.*

Abney (Captain W. de W., R.E., F.R.S.) Thebes, and its Five Greater Temples. Forty large Permanent Photographs, with descriptive letter-press. Super-royal 4to, cloth extra, 63*s.*

About Some Fellows. By an ETON BOY, Author of "A Day of my Life." Cloth limp, square 16mo, 2*s.* 6*d.*

Adventures of Captain Mago. A Phœnician's Explorations 1000 years B.C. By LEON CAHUN. Numerous Illustrations. Crown 8vo, cloth extra, gilt, 7*s.* 6*d.*

Adventures of a Young Naturalist. By LUCIEN BIART, with 117 beautiful Illustrations on Wood. Edited and adapted by PARKER GILLMORE. Post 8vo, cloth extra, gilt edges, New Edition, 7*s.* 6*d.*

Adventures in New Guinea. The Narrative of the Captivity of a French Sailor for Nine Years among the Savages in the Interior. Small post 8vo, with Illustrations and Map, cloth, gilt, 6*s.*

Africa, and the Brussels Geographical Conference. Translated from the French of EMILE BANNING, by R. H. MAJOR, F.S.A. With Map, crown 8vo, 7*s.* 6*d.*

Alcott (Louisa M.) Aunt Jo's Scrap-Bag. Square 16mo, 2*s.* 6*d.* (Rose Library, 1*s.*)

——— *Cupid and Chow-Chow.* Small post 8vo, 3*s.* 6*d.*

——— *Little Men: Life at Plumfield with Jo's Boys.* Small post 8vo, cloth, gilt edges, 3*s.* 6*d.* (Rose Library, Double vol. 2*s.*)

——— *Little Women.* 1 vol., cloth, gilt edges, 3*s.* 6*d.* (Rose Library, 2 vols., 1*s.* each.)

A

Beumer's German Copybooks.   In six gradations at 4*d.* each.

Biart (Lucien).   See "Adventures of a Young Naturalist."
"My Rambles in the New World," "The Two Friends."

Bickersteth's Hymnal Companion to Book of Common Prayer.
The Original Editions, containing 403 Hymns, always kept in Print.

Revised and Enlarged Edition, containing 550 Hymns—

** The Revised Editions are entirely distinct from, and cannot be used with, the original editions.

				s.	d
7A	Medium 32mo, cloth limp			0	8
7B	ditto	roan		1	2
7C	ditto	morocco or calf		2	6
8A	Super-royal 32mo, cloth limp			1	0
8B	ditto	red edges		1	2
8C	ditto	roan		2	2
8D	ditto	morocco or calf		3	6
9A	Crown 8vo, cloth, red edges			3	0
9B	ditto	roan		4	0
9C	ditto	morocco or calf		6	0
10A	Crown 8vo, with Introduction and Notes, red edges			4	0
10B	ditto	roan		5	0
10C	ditto	morocco		7	6
11A	Penny Edition in Wrapper			0	1
11B	ditto	cloth		0	2
11C	With Prayer Book, cloth			0	9
11D	ditto	roan		1	0
11E	ditto	morocco		2	6
11F	ditto	persian		1	6
12A	Crown 8vo, with Tunes, cloth, plain edges			4	0
12B	ditto	ditto	persian, red edges	6	6
12C	ditto	ditto	limp morocco, gilt edges	7	6
13A	Small 4to, for Organ			8	6
13B	ditto	ditto	limp russia	21	0
	Chant Book Supplement (Music)			1	6
	Ditto	4to, for Organ		3	6
14A	Tonic Sol-fa Edition			3	6
14B	ditto	treble and alto only		1	0
5B	Chants only			1	6
5D	ditto	4to, for Organ		3	6
	The Church Mission Hymn-Book		*per* 100	8	4
	Ditto	ditto	cloth	*each* 0	4

The "Hymnal Companion" may now be had in special bindings for presentation with and without the Common Prayer Book. A red line edition is ready. Lists on application.

Bickersteth (Rev. E. H., M.A.) The Reef and other Parables.
· 1 vol., square 8vo, with numerous very beautiful Engravings, 7*s.* 6*d.*

—————— *The Clergyman in his Home.*   Small post 8vo, 1*s.*

Bickersteth (Rev. E. H., M.A.) The Master's Home-Call; or, Brief Memorials of Alice Frances Bickersteth. 20th Thousand. 32mo, cloth gilt, 1s.

"They recall in a touching manner a character of which the religious beauty has a warmth and grace almost too tender to be definite."—*The Guardian.*

———— *The Shadow of the Rock.* A Selection of Religious Poetry. 18mo, cloth extra, 2s. 6d.

———— *The Shadowed Home and the Light Beyond.* 7th Edition, crown 8vo, cloth extra, 5s.

Bida. The Authorized Version of the Four Gospels, with the whole of the magnificent Etchings on Steel, after drawings by M. BIDA, in 4 vols., appropriately bound in cloth extra, price 3l. 3s. each.

Also the four volumes in two, bound in the best morocco, by Suttaby, extra gilt edges, 18l. 18s., half-morocco, 12l. 12s.

"Bida's Illustrations of the Gospels of St. Matthew and St. John have already received here and elsewhere a full recognition of their great merits."—*Times.*

Bidwell (C. T.) The Balearic Islands. Illustrations and a Map. Crown 8vo, cloth, 10s. 6d.

———— *The Cost of Living Abroad.* Crown 8vo, 6s.

Black (Wm.) Three Feathers. Small post 8vo, cloth extra, 6s.

———— *Lady Silverdale's Sweetheart, and other Stories.* 1 vol., small post 8vo, 6s.

———— *Kilmeny: a Novel.* Small post 8vo, cloth, 6s.

———— *In Silk Attire.* 3rd Edition, small post 8vo, 6s.

———— *A Daughter of Heth.* 11th Edition, small post 8vo, 6s.

Blackmore (R. D.) Lorna Doone. 10th Edition, cr. 8vo, 6s.

"The reader at times holds his breath, so graphically yet so simply does John Ridd tell his tale."—*Saturday Review.*

———— *Alice Lorraine.* 1 vol., small post 8vo, 6th Edition, 6s.

———— *Clara Vaughan.* Revised Edition, 6s.

———— *Cradock Nowell.* New Edition, 6s.

———— *Cripps the Carrier.* 3rd Edition, small post 8vo, 6s.

Blossoms from the King's Garden : Sermons for Children. By the Rev. C. BOSANQUET. 2nd Edition, small post 8vo, cloth extra, 6s.

Blue Banner (The); or, The Adventures of a Mussulman, a Christian, and a Pagan, in the time of the Crusades and Mongol Conquest. By LEON CAHUN. Translated from the French by W. COLLETT SANDARS. With Seventy-six Wood Engravings. 1 vol., square imperial 16mo, cloth extra, 7s. 6d.

Book of English Elegies. Small post 8vo, cloth extra, 5s.

Book of the Play. By DUTTON COOK. 2 vols., crown 8vo, 24s.

Bradford (Wm.) The Arctic Regions. Illustrated with Photographs, taken on an Art Expedition to Greenland. With Descriptive Narrative by the Artist. In One Volume, royal broadside, 25 inches by 20, beautifully bound in morocco extra, price Twenty-Five Guineas.

Brave Men in Action. By S. J. MACKENNA. Crown 8vo,
480 pp., cloth, 10s. 6d.

Breck (Samuel). *See* " Recollections."

Browning (Mrs. E. B.) The Rhyme of the Duchess May.
Demy 4to, Illustrated with Eight Photographs, after Drawings by
CHARLOTTE M. B. MORRELL. 21s.

Bryant (W. C., assisted by S. H. Gay) A Popular History of
the United States. About 4 vols., to be profusely Illustrated with
Engravings on Steel and Wood, after Designs by the best Artists.
Vol. I., super-royal 8vo, cloth extra, gilt, 42s., is ready.

Burnaby (Capt.) See " On Horseback."

Burton (Captain R. F.) Two Trips to Gorilla Land and the
Cataracts of the Congo. By Captain R. F. BURTON. 2 vols, demy
8vo, with numerous Illustrations and Map, cloth extra, 28s.

Butler (W. F.) The Great Lone Land; an·Account of the Red
River Expedition, 1869-70, and Subsequent Travels and Adventures
in the Manitoba Country, and a Winter Journey across the Saskatche-
wan Valley to the Rocky Mountains. With Illustrations and Map.
Fifth and Cheaper Edition, crown 8vo, cloth extra, 7s. 6d.

—— *The Wild North Land; the Story of a Winter*
Journey with Dogs across Northern North America. Demy 8vo, cloth,
with numerous Woodcuts and a Map, 4th Edition, 18s. Cr. 8vo, 7s. 6d.

—— *Akim-foo: the History of a Failure.* Demy 8vo, cloth,
2nd Edition, 16s. Also, in crown 8vo, 7s. 6d.

By Land and Ocean; or, The Journal and Letters of a Tour
round the World by a Young Girl, who went *alone* to Victoria, New
Zealand, Sydney, Singapore, China, Japan, and across the Continent
of America home. By F. L. RAINS. Crown 8vo, cloth, 7s. 6d.

CABUL: the Ameer, his Country, and his People. By PHIL
ROBINSON, Special Correspondent of the *Daily Telegraph*, with the
Army of Afghanistan. With a Portrait of Shere Ali, and a Map of
the Seat of the Anglo-Russian Question. 16mo, 1s. Fourth Thousand.

Cadogan (Lady A.) Illustrated Games of Patience. Twenty-
four Diagrams in Colours, with Descriptive Text. Foolscap 4to,
cloth extra, gilt edges, 3rd Edition, 12s. 6d.

Cahun (Leon) Adventures of Captain Mago. *See* " Adventures."

—— *Blue Banner*, which see.

Carbon Process (A Manual of). *See* LIESEGANG.

Ceramic Art. *See* JACQUEMART.

Changed Cross (The), and other Religious Poems. 16mo, 2s. 6d.

Child of the Cavern (The); or, Strange Doings Underground.
By JULES VERNE. Translated by W. H. G. KINGSTON, Author of
" Snow Shoes and Canoes," " Peter the Whaler," " The Three
Midshipmen," &c., &c., &c. Numerous Illustrations. Square crown
8vo, cloth extra, gilt edges, 7s. 6d.

Child's Play, with 16 Coloured Drawings by E. V. B. Printed on thick paper, with tints, 7s. 6d.

———— *New.* By E. V. B. Similar to the above. *See* New.

Chips from many Blocks. By ELIHU BURRITT, Author of "Walks in the Black Country," "From London to Land's End," "Sparks from the Anvil," &c. Demy 8vo, cloth extra, 6s.

Choice Editions of Choice Books. 2s. 6d. each, Illustrated by C. W. COPE, R.A., T. CRESWICK, R.A., E. DUNCAN, BIRKET FOSTER, J. C. HORSLEY, A.R.A., G. HICKS, R. REDGRAVE, R.A., C. STONEHOUSE, F. TAYLER, G. THOMAS, H. J. TOWNSHEND, E. H. WEHNERT, HARRISON WEIR, &c.

Bloomfield's Farmer's Boy.	Milton's L'Allegro.
Campbell's Pleasures of Hope.	Poetry of Nature. Harrison Weir.
Coleridge's Ancient Mariner.	Rogers' (Sam.) Pleasures of Memory.
Goldsmith's Deserted Village.	Shakespeare's Songs and Sonnets.
Goldsmith's Vicar of Wakefield.	Tennyson's May Queen.
Gray's Elegy in a Churchyard.	Elizabethan Poets.
Keat's Eve of St. Agnes.	Wordsworth's Pastoral Poems.

"Such works are a glorious beatification for a poet."—*Athenæum.*

Christian Activity. By ELEANOR C. PRICE. Cloth extra, 6s.

Christmas Story-teller (The). By Old Hands and New Ones. Crown 8vo, cloth extra, gilt edges, Fifty-two Illustrations, 10s. 6d.

Cobbett (William). A Biography. By EDWARD SMITH. 2 vols., crown 8vo, 25s.

Cook (D.) Young Mr. Nightingale. A Novel. 3 vols., 31s. 6d.

———— *The Banns of Marriage.* 2 vols., crown 8vo, 21s.

———— *Book of the Play.* 2 vols., crown 8vo, 24s.

———— *Doubleday's Children.* 3 vols., crown 8vo, 31s. 6d.

Coope (Col. W. Jesser) A Prisoner of War in Russia. By Col. W. JESSER COOPE, Imperial Ottoman Gendarmerie. Crown 8vo, cloth extra, 10s. 6d.

Covert Side Sketches: Thoughts on Hunting, with Different Packs and in Different Countries. By J. NEVITT FITT (H.H. of the *Sporting Gazette*, late of the *Field*). Crown 8vo, cloth extra, 10s. 6d.

Craik (Mrs.) The Adventures of a Brownie. By the Author of "John Halifax, Gentleman." With numerous Illustrations by Miss PATERSON. Square cloth, extra gilt edges, 5s.

Cripps the Carrier. 3rd Edition, 6s. *See* BLACKMORE.

Cruise of H.M.S. "Challenger" (The). By W. J. J. SPRY, R.N. With Route Map and many Illustrations. 6th Edition, demy 8vo, cloth, 18s. Cheap Edition, crown 8vo, small type, some of the Illustrations, 7s. 6d.

"The book before us supplies the information in a manner that leaves little to be desired. 'The Cruise of H.M.S. *Challenger*' is an exceedingly well-written, entertaining, and instructive book."—*United Service Gazette.*

"Agreeably written, full of information, and copiously illustrated." — *Broad Arrow.*

Curious Adventures of a Field Cricket. By Dr. ERNEST
CANDÈZE. Translated by N. D'ANVERS. With numerous fine
Illustrations. Crown 8vo, cloth extra, gilt edges, 7*s.* 6*d.*

DANA (R. H.) Two Years before the Mast and Twenty-Four
years After. Revised Edition with Notes, 12mo, 6*s.*

Dana (Jas. D.) Corals and Coral Islands. Numerous Illustrations, Charts, &c. New and Cheaper Edition, with numerous
important Additions and Corrections. Crown 8vo, cloth extra, 8*s.* 6*d.*

Daughter (A) of Heth. By W. BLACK. Crown 8vo, 6*s.*

Day of My Life (A) ; or, Every Day Experiences at Eton.
By an ETON BOY, Author of "About Some Fellows." 16mo, cloth
extra, 2*s.* 6*d.* 6th Thousand.

Dick Sands, the Boy Captain. By JULES VERNE. With
nearly 100 Illustrations, cloth extra, gilt edges, 10*s.* 6*d.*

Discoveries of Prince Henry the Navigator, and their Results ;
being the Narrative of the Discovery by Sea, within One Century, of
more than Half the World. By RICHARD HENRY MAJOR, F.S.A.
Demy 8vo, with several Woodcuts, 4 Maps, and a Portrait of Prince
Henry in Colours. Cloth extra, 15*s.*

Dodge (Mrs. M.) Hans Brinker; or, the Silver Skates. An
entirely New Edition, with 59 Full-page and other Woodcuts.
Square crown 8vo, cloth extra, 7*s.* 6*d.* ; Text only, paper, 1*s.*

———— *Theophilus and Others.* 1 vol., small post 8vo, cloth
extra, gilt, 3*s.* 6*d.*

Dogs of Assize. A Legal Sketch-Book in Black and White.
Containing 6 Drawings by WALTER J. ALLEN. · Folio, in wrapper,
6*s.* 8*d.*

Doré's Spain. *See* "Spain."

Dougall's (J. D.) Shooting; its Appliances, Practice, and
Purpose. With Illustrations, cloth extra, 10*s.* 6*d.* *See* "Shooting."

EARLY History of the Colony of Victoria (The), from its
Discovery to its Establishment as a Self-Governing Province of the
British Empire. By FRANCIS P. LABILLIERE, Fellow of the Royal
Colonial Institute, &c. 2 vols., crown 8vo, 21*s.*

Echoes of the Heart. *See* MOODY.

Elinor Dryden. By Mrs. MACQUOID. Crown 8vo, 6*s.*

English Catalogue of Books (The). Published during 1863 to
1871 inclusive, comprising also important American Publications.
This Volume, occupying over 450 Pages, shows the Titles of
32,000 New Books and New Editions issued during Nine Years, with
the Size, Price, and Publisher's Name, the Lists of Learned Societies,
Printing Clubs, and other Literary Associations, and the Books
issued by them; as also the Publisher's Series and Collections—
altogether forming an indispensable adjunct to the Bookseller's

Establishment, as well as to every Learned and Literary Club and Association. 30*s.*, half-bound.

** Of the previous Volume, 1835 to 1862, very few remain on sale; as also of the Index Volume, 1837 to 1857.

English Catalogue of Books (The) Supplements, 1863, 1864, 1865, 3*s.* 6*d.* each; 1866, 1867, to 1878, 5*s.* each.

Eight Cousins. See ALCOTT.

English Writers, Chapters for Self-Improvement in English Literature. By the Author of "The Gentle Life," 6*s.*

Eton. See "Day of my Life," "Out of School," "About Some Fellows."

Evans (C.) Over the Hills and Far Away. By C. EVANS. One Volume, crown 8vo, cloth extra, 10*s.* 6*d.*

——— *A Strange Friendship.* Crown 8vo, cloth, 5*s.*

FAITH Gartney's Girlhood. By the Author of "The Gayworthy's." Fcap. with Coloured Frontispiece, 3*s.* 6*d.*

Familiar Letters on some Mysteries of Nature. See PHIPSON.

Favourite English Pictures. Containing Sixteen Permanent Autotype Reproductions of important Paintings of Modern British Artists. With letterpress descriptions. Atlas 4to, cloth extra, 2*l.* 2*s.*

Fern Paradise (The): A Plea for the Culture of Ferns. By F. G. HEATH. New Edition, entirely Rewritten, Illustrated with eighteen full-page and numerous other Woodcuts, and four permanent Photographs, large post 8vo, handsomely bound in cloth, 12*s.* 6*d.*

Fern World (The). By F. G. HEATH. Illustrated by Twelve Coloured Plates, giving complete Figures (Sixty-four in all) of every Species of British Fern, specially printed from Nature; by several full-page Engravings; and a permanent Photograph. Large post 8vo., cloth, gilt edges, 400 pp., 4th Edition, 12*s.* 6*d.*

Few (A) Hints on Proving Wills. Enlarged Edition, 1*s.*

Five Weeks in Greece. By J. F. YOUNG. Crown 8vo, 10*s.* 6*d.*

Flammarion (C.) The Atmosphere. Translated from the French of CAMILLE FLAMMARION. Edited by JAMES GLAISHER, F.R.S., Superintendent of the Magnetical and Meteorological Department of the Royal Observatory at Greenwich. With 10 Chromo-Lithographs and 81 Woodcuts. Royal 8vo, cloth extra, 30*s.*

Flooding of the Sahara (The). An Account of the project for opening direct communication with 38,000,000 people. With a description of North-West Africa and Soudan. By DONALD MACKENZIE. 8vo, cloth extra, with Illustrations, 10*s.* 6*d.*

Footsteps of the Master. See STOWE (Mrs. BEECHER).

Forrest (John) Explorations in Australia. Being Mr. JOHN FORREST's Personal Account of his Journeys. 1 vol., demy 8vo, cloth, with several Illustrations and 3 Maps, 16*s.*

Franc (Maude Jeane). The following form one Series, small post 8vo, in uniform cloth bindings:—

—— *Emily's Choice.* 5s.

—— *Hall's Vineyard.* 4s.

—— *John's Wife: a Story of Life in South Australia.* 4s.

——- *Marian ; or, the Light of Some One's Home.* 5s.

—— *Silken Cords and Iron Fetters.* 4s.

—— *Vermont Vale.* 5s.

—— *Minnie's Mission.* 4s.

—— *Little Mercy.* 5s.

French Heiress (A) in her own Chateau. Crown 8vo, 12s. 6d.

Funny Foreigners and Eccentric Englishmen. 16 coloured comic Illustrations for Children. Fcap. folio, coloured wrappper, 4s.

GAMES of Patience. See CADOGAN.

Garvagh (Lord) The Pilgrim of Scandinavia. By LORD GARVAGH, B.A., Christ Church, Oxford, and Member of the Alpine Club. 8vo, cloth extra, with Illustrations, 10s. 6d.

Geary (Grattan). See "Asiatic Turkey."

Gentle Life (Queen Edition). 2 vols. in 1, small 4to, 10s. 6d.

THE GENTLE LIFE SERIES.

Price 6s. each ; or in calf extra, price 10s. 6d.

The Gentle Life. Essays in aid of the Formation of Character of Gentlemen and Gentlewomen. 21st Edition.

" Deserves to be printed in letters of gold, and circulated in every house."—*Chambers' Journal.*

About in the World. Essays by the Author of "The Gentle Life."

" It is not easy to open it at any page without finding some handy idea."—*Morning Post.*

Like unto Christ. A New Translation of Thomas à Kempis' " De Imitatione Christi." With a Vignette from an Original Drawing by Sir THOMAS LAWRENCE. 2nd Edition.

" Could not be presented in a more exquisite form, for a more sightly volume was never seen."—*Illustrated London News.*

Familiar Words. An Index Verborum, or Quotation Handbook. Affording an immediate Reference to Phrases and Sentences that have become embedded in the English language. 3rd and enlarged Edition.

" The most extensive dictionary of quotation we have met with."—*Notes and Queries.*

The Gentle Life Series, continued :—

Essays by Montaigne. Edited, Compared, Revised, and Annotated by the Author of "The Gentle Life." With Vignette Portrait. 2nd Edition.

"We should be glad if any words of ours could help to bespeak a large circulation for this handsome attractive book."—*Illustrated Times.*

The Countess of Pembroke's Arcadia. Written by Sir PHILIP SIDNEY. Edited with Notes by Author of "The Gentle Life." 7s. 6d.

"All the best things in the Arcadia are retained intact in Mr. Friswell's edition." —*Examiner.*

The Gentle Life. 2nd Series, 8th Edition.

"There is not a single thought in the volume that does not contribute in some measure to the formation of a true gentleman."—*Daily News.*

Varia : Readings from Rare Books. Reprinted, by permission, from the *Saturday Review, Spectator*, &c.

"The books discussed in this volume are no less valuable than they are rare, and the compiler is entitled to the gratitude of the public."—*Observer.*

The Silent Hour : Essays, Original and Selected. By the Author of "The Gentle Life." 3rd Edition.

"All who possess 'The Gentle Life' should own this volume."—*Standard.*

Half-Length Portraits. Short Studies of Notable Persons. By J. HAIN FRISWELL. Small post 8vo, cloth extra, 6s.

Essays on English Writers, for the Self-improvement of Students in English Literature.

"To all (both men and women) who have neglected to read and study their native literature we would certainly suggest the volume before us as a fitting introduction." —*Examiner.*

Other People's Windows. By J. HAIN FRISWELL. 3rd Edition.

"The chapters are so lively in themselves, so mingled with shrewd views of human nature, so full of illustrative anecdotes, that the reader cannot fail to be amused."—*Morning Post.*

A Man's Thoughts. By J. HAIN FRISWELL.

German Primer. Being an Introduction to First Steps in German. By M. T. PREU. 2s. 6d.

Getting On in the World ; or, Hints on Success in Life. By W. MATHEWS, LL.D. Small post 8vo, cloth, 2s. 6d.; gilt edges, 3s. 6d.

Gouffé. The Royal Cookery Book. By JULES GOUFFÉ; translated and adapted for English use by ALPHONSE GOUFFÉ, Head Pastrycook to her Majesty the Queen. Illustrated with large plates printed in colours. 161 Woodcuts, 8vo, cloth extra, gilt edges, 2l. 2s.

—— Domestic Edition, half-bound, 10s. 6d.

"By far the ablest and most complete work on cookery that has ever been submitted to the gastronomical world."—*Pall Mall Gazette.*

—— *The Book of Preserves ; or, Receipts for Preparing and Preserving Meat,* Fish salt and smoked, Terrines, Gelatines, Vegetables, Fruit, Confitures, Syrups, Liqueurs de Famille, Petits Fours, Bonbons, &c., &c. 1 vol., royal 8vo, containing upwards of 500 Receipts and 34 Illustrations, 10s. 6d.

Gouffé. Royal Book of Pastry and Confectionery. By JULES GOUFFÉ, Chef-de-Cuisine of the Paris Jockey Club. Royal 8vo, Illustrated with 10 Chromo-lithographs and 137 Woodcuts, from Drawings by E. MONJAT. Cloth extra, gilt edges, 35*s.*

Gouraud (Mdlle.) Four Gold Pieces. Numerous Illustrations. Small post 8vo, cloth, 2*s.* 6*d.* *See also* Rose Library.

Government of M. Thiers. By JULES SIMON. Translated from the French. 2 vols., demy 8vo, cloth extra.

Gower (Lord Ronald) Handbook to the Art Galleries, Public and Private, of Belgium and Holland. 18mo, cloth, 5*s.*

—————— *The Castle Howard Portraits.* 2 vols., folio, cl. extra, 6*l.* 6*s.*

Greek Grammar. *See* WALLER.

Guizot's History of France. Translated by ROBERT BLACK. Super-royal 8vo, very numerous Full-page and other Illustrations. In 5 vols., cloth extra, gilt, each 24*s.*

"It supplies a want which has long been felt, and ought to be in the hands of all students of history."—*Times.*

"Three-fourths of M. Guizot's great work are now completed, and the 'History of France,' which was so nobly planned, has been hitherto no less admirably executed."—*From long Review of Vol. III. in the Times.*

"M. Guizot's main merit is this, that, in a style at once clear and vigorous, he sketches the essential and most characteristic features of the times and personages described, and seizes upon every salient point which can best illustrate and bring out to view what is most significant and instructive in the spirit of the age described."—*Evening Standard,* Sept. 23, 1874.

—————— *History of England.* In 3 vols. of about 500 pp. each, containing 60 to 70 Full-page and other Illustrations, cloth extra, gilt, 24*s.* each. Vol. III. in the press.

"For luxury of typography, plainness of print, and beauty of illustration, these volumes, of which but one has as yet appeared in English, will hold their own against any production of an age so luxurious as our own in everything, typography not excepted."—*Times.*

Guillemin. *See* "World of Comets."

Guyon (Mde.) Life. By UPHAM. 6th Edition, crown 8vo, 6*s.*

Guyot (A.) Physical Geography. By ARNOLD GUYOT, Author of "Earth and Man." In 1 volume, large 4to, 128 pp., numerous coloured Diagrams, Maps, and Woodcuts, price 10*s.* 6*d.*

HABITATIONS of Man in all Ages. *See* LE-DUC.

Hamilton (A. H. A., J.P.) *See* "Quarter Sessions."

Handbook to the Charities of London. *See* Low's.

—————— *Principal Schools of England.* *See* Practical.

Half-Hours of Blind Man's Holiday; or, Summer and Winter Sketches in Black & White. By W. W. FENN. 2 vols., cr. 8vo, 24*s.*

Half-Length Portraits. Short Studies of Notable Persons. By J. HAIN FRISWELL. Small post 8vo, cloth extra, 6*s.*

Hall (W. W.) How to Live Long; or, 1408 Health Maxims, Physical, Mental, and Moral. By W. W. HALL, A.M., M.D. Small post 8vo, cloth, 2*s.* Second Edition.

Hans Brinker; or, the Silver Skates. *See* DODGE.

Healy (M.) A Summer's Romance. Crown 8vo, cloth, 10s. 6d.

——— *The Home Theatre.* Small post 8vo, 3s. 6d.

Heart of Africa. Three Years' Travels and Adventures in the Unexplored Regions of Central Africa, from 1868 to 1871. By Dr. GEORG SCHWEINFURTH. Translated by ELLEN E. FREWER. With an Introduction by WINWOOD READE. An entirely New Edition, revised and condensed by the Author. Numerous Illustrations, and large Map. 2 vols., crown 8vo, cloth, 15s.

Heath (F. G.). See "Fern World," "Fern Paradise," "Our Woodland Trees."

Heber's (Bishop) Illustrated Edition of Hymns. With upwards of 100 beautiful Engravings. Small 4to, handsomely bound, 7s. 6d. Morocco, 18s. 6d. and 21s. An entirely New Edition.

Hector Servadac. See VERNE. The heroes of this story were carried away through space on the Comet "Gallia," and their adventures are recorded with all Jules Verne's characteristic spirit. With nearly 100 Illustrations, cloth extra, gilt edges, 10s. 6d.

Henderson (A.) Latin Proverbs and Quotations; with Translations and Parallel Passages, and a copious English Index. By ALFRED HENDERSON. Fcap. 4to, 530 pp., 10s. 6d.

History and Handbook of Photography. Translated from the French of GASTON TISSANDIER. Edited by J. THOMSON. Imperial 16mo, over 300 pages, 70 Woodcuts, and Specimens of Prints by the best Permanent Processes, cloth extra, 6s. Second Edition, with an Appendix by the late Mr. HENRY FOX TALBOT, giving an account of his researches.

History of a Crime (The); Deposition of an Eye-witness. By VICTOR HUGO. 4 vols., crown 8vo, 42s.

——— *England. See* GUIZOT.

——— *France. See* GUIZOT.

——— *Russia. See* RAMBAUD.

——— *Merchant Shipping. See* LINDSAY.

——— *United States. See* BRYANT.

——— *Ireland.* By STANDISH O'GRADY. Vol. I. ready, 7s. 6d.

History and Principles of Weaving by Hand and by Power. With several hundred Illustrations. Reprinted with considerable additions from "Engineering," with a chapter on Lace making Machinery. By ALFRED BARLOW. Royal 8vo, cloth extra, 1l. 5s.

Hitherto. By the Author of "The Gayworthys." New Edition, cloth extra, 3s. 6d. Also, in Rose Library, 2 vols., 2s.

Hofmann (Carl). A Practical Treatise on the Manufacture of Paper in all its Branches. Illustrated by 110 Wood Engravings, and 5 large Folding Plates. In 1 vol., 4to, cloth; about 400 pp., 3l. 13s. 6d.

How to Build a House.   See LE-DUC.

How to Live Long.   See HALL.

Hugo (Victor) "*Ninety-Three.*"   Illustrated.   Crown 8vo, 6s.

———— *Toilers of the Sea.*   Crown 8vo.   Illustrated, 6s. ; fancy
boards, 2s. ; cloth, 2s. 6d. ; On large paper with all the original
Illustrations, 10s. 6d.

———— *See* "History of a Crime."

Hunting, Shooting, and Fishing ; A Sporting Miscellany.
Illustrated.   Crown 8vo, cloth extra, 7s. 6d.

Hymnal Companion to Book of Common Prayer.   See
BICKERSTETH.

ILLUSTRATIONS of China and its People.   By J.
THOMSON, F.R.G.S.   Being 200 permanent Photographs from the
Author's Negatives, with Letterpress Descriptions of the Places and
People represented.   Four Volumes imperial 4to, each 3l. 3s.

In my Indian Garden.   By PHIL. ROBINSON.   With a Preface
by EDWIN ARNOLD, M.A., C.S.I., &c.   Crown 8vo, limp cloth, 3s. 6d.

Irish Bar.   Comprising Anecdotes, Bon-Mots, and Biographical Sketches of the Bench and Bar of Ireland.   By J. RODERICK
O'FLANAGAN, Barrister-at-Law.   1 vol., crown 8vo, cloth.

JACQUEMART (A.) History of the Ceramic Art : Descriptive and Analytical Study of the Potteries of all Times and of
all Nations.   By ALBERT JACQUEMART.   200 Woodcuts by H.
Catenacci and J. Jacquemart.   12 Steel-plate Engravings, and 1000
Marks and Monograms.   Translated by Mrs. BURY PALLISER.   In
1 vol., super-royal 8vo, of about 700 pp., cloth extra, gilt edges, 28s.
"This is one of those few gift-books which, while they can certainly lie on a table
and look beautiful, can also be read through with real pleasure and profit."—*Times.*

KENNEDY'S (Capt. W. R.) Sporting Adventures in the
Pacific.   With Illustrations, demy 8vo, 18s.

———— *(Capt. A. W. M. Clark).*   *See* "To the Arctic
Regions."

Khedive's Egypt (The) ; or, The old House of Bondage under
New Masters.   By EDWIN DE LEON, Ex-Agent and Consul-General
in Egypt.   In 1 vol., demy 8vo, cloth extra, Third Edition, 18s.

Kingston (W. H. G.).   See "Snow-Shoes."

———— *Child of the Cavern.*

———— *Two Supercargoes.*

———— *With Axe and Rifle.*

Koldewey (Capt.) The Second North German Polar Expedition
in the Year 1869-70, of the Ships "Germania" and "Honsa," under
command of Captain Koldewey.   Edited and condensed by H. W.
BATES, Esq.   Numerous Woodcuts, Maps, and Chromo-lithographs.
Royal 8vo, cloth extra, 1l. 15s.

LADY Silverdale's Sweetheart. 6s. *See* BLACK.

Land of Bolivar (The) ; or, War, Peace, and Adventure in the Republic of Venezuela. By JAMES MUDIE SPENCE, F.R.G.S., F.Z.S. 2 vols., demy 8vo, cloth extra, with numerous Woodcuts and Maps, 31s. 6d. Second Edition.

Landseer Gallery (The). Containing thirty-six Autotype Reproductions of Engravings from the most important early works of Sir EDWIN LANDSEER. With a Memoir of the Artist's Life, and Descriptions of the Plates. Imperial 4to, handsomely bound in cloth, gilt edges, 2l. 2s.

Le-Duc (V.) How to build a House. By VIOLLET-LE-DUC, Author of "The Dictionary of Architecture," &c. Numerous Illustrations, Plans, &c. Medium 8vo, cloth, gilt, 12s.

——— *Annals of a Fortress.* Numerous Illustrations and Diagrams. Demy 8vo, cloth extra, 15s.

——— *The Habitations of Man in all Ages.* By E. VIOLLET-LE-DUC. Illustrated by 103 Woodcuts. Translated by BENJAMIN BUCKNALL, Architect. 8vo, cloth extra, 16s.

——— *Lectures on Architecture.* By VIOLLET-LE-DUC. Translated from the French by BENJAMIN BUCKNALL, Architect. In 2 vols., royal 8vo, 3l. 3s. Also in Parts, 10s. 6d. each.

——— *Mont Blanc: a Treatise on its Geodesical and Geo-*logical Constitution—its Transformations, and the Old and Modern state of its Glaciers. By EUGENE VIOLLET-LE-DUC. With 120 Illustrations. Translated by B. BUCKNALL. 1 vol., demy 8vo, 14s.

——— *On Restoration;* with a Notice of his Works by CHARLES WETHERED. Crown 8vo, with a Portrait on Steel of VIOLLET-LE DUC, cloth extra, 2s. 6d.

Lenten Meditations. In Two Series, each complete in itself. By the Rev. CLAUDE BOSANQUET, Author of "Blossoms from the King's Garden." 16mo, cloth, First Series, 1s. 6d. ; Second Series, 2s.

Liesegang (Dr. Paul E.) A Manual of the Carbon Process of Photography, and its use in Making Enlargements, &c. Translated from the Sixth German Edition by R. B. MARSTON. Demy 8vo, half-bound, with Illustrations, 4s.

Life and Letters of the Honourable Charles Sumner (The). 2 vols., royal 8vo, cloth. The Letters give full description of London Society—Lawyers—Judges—Visits to Lords Fitzwilliam, Leicester, Wharncliffe, Brougham—Association with Sydney Smith, Hallam, Macaulay, Dean Milman, Rogers, and Talfourd ; also, a full Journal which Sumner kept in Paris. Second Edition, 36s.

Lindsay (W. S.) History of Merchant Shipping and Ancient Commerce. Over 150 Illustrations, Maps and Charts. In 4 vols., demy 8vo, cloth extra. Vols. 1 and 2, 21s. ; vols. 3 and 4, 24s. each.

Lion Jack: a Story of Perilous Adventures amongst Wild Men and Beasts. Showing how Menageries are made. By P. T. BARNUM. With Illustrations. Crown 8vo, cloth extra, price 6s.

Little King; or, the Taming of a Young Russian Count. By S. BLANDY. Translated from the French. 64 Illustrations. Crown 8vo, cloth extra, gilt, 7s. 6d.

Little Mercy; or, For Better for Worse. By MAUDE JEANNE FRANC, Author of "Marian," "Vermont Vale," &c., &c. Small post 8vo, cloth extra, 4s.

Locker (A.) The Village Surgeon. A Fragment of Auto-biography. By ARTHUR LOCKER. Crown 8vo, cloth, 3s. 6d.

Long (Col. C. Chaillé) Central Africa. Naked Truths of Naked People : an Account of Expeditions to Lake Victoria Nyanza and the Mabraka Niam-Niam. Demy 8vo, numerous Illustrations, 18s.

Lord Collingwood: a Biographical Study. By. W. DAVIS. With Steel Engraving of Lord Collingwood. Crown 8vo, 2s.

Lost Sir Massingberd. New Edition, 16mo, boards, coloured wrapper, 2s.

Low's German Series—

1. **The Illustrated German Primer.** Being the easiest introduction to the study of German for all beginners. 1s.
2. **The Children's own German Book.** A Selection of Amusing and Instructive Stories in Prose. Edited by Dr. A. L. MEISSNER, Professor of Modern Languages in the Queen's University in Ireland. Small post 8vo, cloth, 1s. 6d.
3. **The First German Reader, for Children from Ten to** Fourteen. Edited by Dr. A. L. MEISSNER. Small post 8vo, cloth, 1s. 6d.
4. **The Second German Reader.** Edited by Dr. A. L. MEISSNER, Small post 8vo, cloth, 1s. 6d.

   Buchheim's Deutsche Prosa. Two Volumes, sold separately :—

5. **Schiller's Prosa.** Containing Selections from the Prose Works of Schiller, with Notes for English Students. By Dr. BUCHHEIM, Professor of the German Language and Literature, King's College, London. Small post 8vo, 2s. 6d.
6. **Goethe's Prosa.** Containing Selections from the Prose Works of Goethe, with Notes for English Students. By Dr. BUCHHEIM. Small post 8vo, 3s. 6d.

Low's Standard Library of Travel and Adventure. Crown 8vo, bound uniformly in cloth extra, price 7s. 6d.

1. **The Great Lone Land.** By W. F. BUTLER, C.B.
2. **The Wild North Land.** By W. F. BUTLER, C.B.
3. **How I found Livingstone.** By H. M. STANLEY.
4. **The Threshold of the Unknown Region.** By C. R. MARK-HAM. (4th Edition, with Additional Chapters, 10s. 6d.)
5. **A Whaling Cruise to Baffin's Bay and the Gulf of Boothia.** By A. H. MARKHAM.

Low's Standard Library of Travel and Adventure, continued :—

   6. **Campaigning on the Oxus.** By J. A. MacGahan.
   7. **Akim-foo : the History of a Failure.** By Major W. F. Butler, C.B.
   8. **Ocean to Ocean.** By the Rev. George M. Grant. With Illustrations.
   9. **Cruise of the Challenger.** By W. J. J. Spry, R.N.
 10. **Schweinfurth's Heart of Africa.** 2 vols., 15*s.*

Low's Standard Novels. Crown 8vo, 6*s.* each, cloth extra.

Three Feathers. By William Black.
A Daughter of Heth. 13th Edition. By W. Black. With Frontispiece by F. Walker, A.R.A.
Kilmeny. A Novel. By W. Black.
In Silk Attire. By W. Black.
Lady Silverdale's Sweetheart. By W. Black.
Alice Lorraine. By R. D. Blackmore.
Lorna Doone. By R. D. Blackmore. 8th Edition.
Cradock Nowell. By R. D. Blackmore.
Clara Vaughan. By R. D. Blackmore.
Cripps the Carrier. By R. D. Blackmore.
Innocent. By Mrs. Oliphant. Eight Illustrations.
Work. A Story of Experience. By Louisa M. Alcott. Illustrations. *See also* Rose Library.
Mistress Judith. A Cambridgeshire Story. By C. C. Fraser-Tytler.
Never Again. By Dr. Mayo, Author of "Kaloolah."
Ninety-Three. By Victor Hugo. Numerous Illustrations.
My Wife and I. By Mrs. Beecher Stowe.
Wreck of the Grosvenor. By W. Clark Russell.
Elinor Dryden. By Mrs. Macquoid.

Low's Handbook to the Charities of London for 1877. Edited and revised to July, 1877, by C. Mackeson, F.S.S., Editor of "A Guide to the Churches of London and its Suburbs," &c. 1*s.*

MACGAHAN (J. A.) Campaigning on the Oxus, and the Fall of Khiva. With Map and numerous Illustrations, 4th Edition, small post 8vo, cloth extra, 7*s.* 6*d.*

——— *Under the Northern Lights ; or, the Cruise of the* "Pandora" to Peel's Straits, in Search of Sir John Franklin's Papers. With Illustrations by Mr. De Wylde, who accompanied the Expedition. Demy 8vo, cloth extra, 18*s.*

Macgregor (John) "Rob Roy" on the Baltic. 3rd Edition, small post 8vo, 2*s.* 6*d.*

——— *A Thousand Miles in the "Rob Roy" Canoe.* 11th Edition, small post 8vo, 2*s.* 6*d.*

——— *Description of the "Rob Roy" Canoe,* with Plans, &c., 1*s.*

——— *The Voyage Alone in the Yawl "Rob Roy."* New Edition, thoroughly revised, with additions, small post 8vo, 5*s.*

Rose Library (The), continued :—

6. **The Old-Fashioned Girl.** By LOUISA M. ALCOTT. Double vol., 2s. ; cloth, 3s. 6d.
7. **The Mistress of the Manse.** By J. G. HOLLAND.
8. **Timothy Titcomb's Letters to Young People, Single and Married.**
9. **Undine, and the Two Captains.** By Baron DE LA MOTTE FOUQUÉ. A New Translation by F. E. BUNNETT. Illustrated.
10. **Draxy Miller's Dowry, and the Elder's Wife.** By SAXE HOLM.
11. **The Four Gold Pieces.** By Madame GOURAUD. Numerous Illustrations.
12. **Work.** A Story of Experience. First Portion. By LOUISA M. ALCOTT.
13. **Beginning Again.** Being a Continuation of "Work." By LOUISA M. ALCOTT.
14. **Picciola;** or, the Prison Flower. By X. B. SAINTINE. Numerous Graphic Illustrations.
15. **Robert's Holidays.** Illustrated.
16. **The Two Children of St. Domingo.** Numerous Illustrations.
17. **Aunt Jo's Scrap Bag.**
18. **Stowe (Mrs. H. B.) The Pearl of Orr's Island.**
19. —— **The Minister's Wooing.**
20. —— **Betty's Bright Idea.**
21. —— **The Ghost in the Mill.**
22. —— **Captain Kidd's Money.**
23. —— **We and our Neighbours.** Double vol., 2s.
24. —— **My Wife and I.** Double vol., 2s. ; cloth, gilt, 3s. 6d.
25. **Hans Brinker;** or, the Silver Skates.
26. **Lowell's My Study Window.**
27. **Holmes (O. W.) The Guardian Angel.**
28. **Warner (C. D.) My Summer in a Garden.**
29. **Hitherto.** By the Author of "The Gayworthys." 2 vols., 1s. each.
30. **Helen's Babies.** By their Latest Victim.
31. **The Barton Experiment.** By the Author of "Helen's Babies."
32. **Dred.** By Mrs. BEECHER STOWE. Double vol., 2s. Cloth, gilt, 3s. 6d.
33. **Warner (C. D.) In the Wilderness.**
34. **Six to One.** A Seaside Story.

Russell (W. H., LL.D.) The Tour of the Prince of Wales in India, and his Visits to the Courts of Greece, Egypt, Spain, and Portugal. By W. H. RUSSELL, LL.D., who accompanied the Prince throughout his journey ; fully Illustrated by SYDNEY P. HALL, M.A., the Prince's Private Artist, with his Royal Highness's special permission to use the Sketches made during the Tour. Super-royal 8vo, cloth extra, gilt edges, 52s. 6d. ; Large Paper Edition, 84s.

SANCTA Christina: a Story of the First Century. By ELEANOR E. ORLEBAR. With a Preface by the Bishop of Winchester. Small post 8vo, cloth extra, 5s.

Schweinfurth (Dr. G.) Heart of Africa. Which see.

—— *Artes Africanæ.* Illustrations and Description of Productions of the Natural Arts of Central African Tribes. With 26 Lithographed Plates, imperial 4to, boards, 28s.

Scientific Memoirs: being Experimental Contributions to a Knowledge of Radiant Energy. By JOHN WILLIAM DRAPER, M.D., LL.D., Author of "A Treatise on Human Physiology," &c. With a fine Steel Engraved Portrait of the Author. Demy 8vo, cloth extra, 473 pages, 14s.

Sea-Gull Rock. By JULES SANDEAU, of the French Academy. Royal 16mo, with 79 Illustrations, cloth extra, gilt edges, 7s. 6d. Cheaper Edition, cloth gilt, 2s. 6d. *See also* Rose Library.

Seonee: Sporting in the Satpura Range of Central India, and in the Valley of the Nerbudda. By R. A. STERNDALE, F.R.G.S. 8vo, with numerous Illustrations, 21s.

Shakespeare (The Boudoir). Edited by HENRY CUNDELL. Carefully bracketted for reading aloud; freed from all objectionable matter, and altogether free from notes. Price 2s. 6d. each volume, cloth extra, gilt edges. Contents :—Vol I., Cymbeline—Merchant of Venice. Each play separately, paper cover, 1s. Vol. II., As You Like It—King Lear—Much Ado about Nothing. Vol. III., Romeo and Juliet—Twelfth Night—King John. The latter six plays separately, paper cover, 9d.

Shooting: its Appliances, Practice, and Purpose. By JAMES DALZIEL DOUGALL, F.S.A., F.Z.A. Author of "Scottish Field Sports," &c. Crown 8vo, cloth extra, 10s. 6d.

"The book is admirable in every way. . . . . We wish it every success "—*Globe.*
"A very complete treatise. . . . . Likely to take high rank as an authority on shooting "—*Daily News.*

Silent Hour (The). *See* Gentle Life Series.

Silver Pitchers. *See* ALCOTT.

Simon (Jules). *See* " Government of M. Thiers."

Six Hundred Robinson Crusoes; or, The Voyage of the Golden Fleece. A true Story for old and young. By GILBERT MORTIMER. Illustrated. Post 8vo, cloth extra, 5s.

Six to One. A Seaside Story. 16mo, boards, 1s.

Sketches from an Artist's Portfolio. By SYDNEY P. HALL. About 60 Fac-similes of his Sketches during Travels in various parts of Europe. Folio, cloth extra, 3l. 3s.

"A portfolio which any one might be glad to call their own."—*Times.*

Sleepy Sketches; or, How we Live, and How we Do Not Live. From Bombay. 1 vol., small post 8vo, cloth, 6s.

" Well-written and amusing sketches of Indian society."—*Morning Post.*

Smith (G.) Assyrian Explorations and Discoveries. By the late GEORGE SMITH. Illustrated by Photographs and Woodcuts. Demy 8vo, 6th Edition, 18s.

Smith (G.) The Chaldean Account of Genesis. Containing the Description of the Creation, the Fall of Man, the Deluge, the Tower of Babel, the Times of the Patriarchs, and Nimrod; Babylonian Fables, and Legends of the Gods; from the Cuneiform Inscriptions. By the late G. SMITH, of the Departmennt of Oriental Antiquities, British Museum. With many Illustrations. Demy 8vo, cloth extra, 5th Edition, 16s.

Snow-Shoes and Canoes; or, the Adventures of a Fur-Hunter in the Hudson's Bay Territory. By W. H. G. KINGSTON. 2nd Edition. With numerous Illustrations. Square crown 8vo, cloth extra, gilt, 7s. 6d.

South Australia: its History, Resources, and Productions. Edited by W. HARCUS, J.P., with 66 full-page Woodcut Illustrations from Photographs taken in the Colony, and 2 Maps. Demy 8vo, 21s.

Spain. Illustrated by GUSTAVE DORÉ. Text by the BARON CH. D'AVILLIER. Containing over 240 Wood Engravings by DORÉ, half of them being Full-page size. Imperial 4to, elaborately bound in cloth, extra gilt edges, 3l. 3s.

Stanley (H. M.) How I Found Livingstone. Crown 8vo, cloth extra, 7s. 6d.; large Paper Edition, 10s. 6d.

———— *"My Kalulu," Prince, King, and Slave.* A Story from Central Africa. Crown 8vo, about 430 pp., with numerous graphic Illustrations, after Original Designs by the Author. Cloth, 7s. 6d.

———— *Coomassie and Magdala.* A Story of Two British Campaigns in Africa. Demy 8vo, with Maps and Illustrations, 16s.

———— *Through the Dark Continent,* which see.

St. Nicholas for 1878. The First Number of the New Series commenced November 1st, 1877, and contains a New Story by LOUISA M. ALCOTT, entitled "Under the Lilacs." 1s. Monthly.

Story without an End. From the German of Carové, by the late Mrs. SARAH T. AUSTIN. Crown 4to, with 15 Exquisite Drawings by E. V. B., printed in Colours in Fac-simile of the original Water Colours; and numerous other Illustrations. New Edition, 7s. 6d.

———— square 4to, with Illustrations by HARVEY. 2s. 6d.

Stowe (Mrs. Beecher) Dred. Cheap Edition, boards, 2s. Cloth, gilt edges, 3s. 6d.

———— *Footsteps of the Master.* With Illustrations and red borders. Small post 8vo, cloth extra, 6s.

———— *Geography,* with 60 Illustrations. Square cloth, 4s. 6d.

———— *Little Foxes.* Cheap Edition, 1s.; Library Edition, 4s. 6d.

———— *Betty's Bright Idea.* 1s.

Stowe (Mrs. Beecher) My Wife and I; or, Harry Henderson's History. Small post 8vo, cloth extra, 6s.*

———— *Minister's Wooing,* 5s.; Copyright Series, 1s. 6d.; cl., 2s.*

———— *Old Town Folk.* 6s.: Cheap Edition, 2s. 6d.

———— *Old Town Fireside Stories.* Cloth extra, 3s. 6d.

———— *Our Folks at Poganuc.* 10s. 6d.

———— *We and our Neighbours.* 1 vol., small post 8vo, 6s. Sequel to "My Wife and I."*

———— *Pink and White Tyranny.* Small post 8vo, 3s. 6d.; Cheap Edition, 1s. 6d. and 2s.

———— *Queer Little People.* 1s.; cloth, 2s.

———— *Chimney Corner.* 1s.; cloth, 1s. 6d.

———— *The Pearl of Orr's Island.* Crown 8vo, 5s.*

———— *Little Pussey Willow.* Fcap., 2s.

———— *Woman in Sacred History.* Illustrated with 15 Chromolithographs and about 200 pages of Letterpress. Demy 4to, cloth extra, gilt edges, 25s.

Street Life in London. By J. THOMSON, F.R.G.S., and ADOLPHE SMITH. One volume, 4to, containing 40 Permanent Photographs of Scenes of London Street Life, with Descriptive Letterpress, 25s.

Student's French Examiner. By F. JULIEN, Author of "Petites Leçons de Conversation et de Grammaire." Square crown 8vo, cloth extra, 2s.

Studies from Nature. 24 Photographs, with Descriptive Letterpress. By STEVEN THOMPSON. Imperial 4to, 35s.

Sub-Tropical Rambles. *See* PIKE (N).

Sullivan (A.M., M.P.). *See* "New Ireland."

Summer Holiday in Scandinavia (A). By E. L. L. ARNOLD. Crown 8vo, cloth extra, 10s. 6d.

Sumner (Hon. Charles). *See* Life and Letters.

Surgeon's Handbook on the Treatment of Wounded in War. By Dr. FRIEDRICH ESMARCH, Professor of Surgery in the University of Kiel, and Surgeon-General to the Prussian Army. Translated by H. H. CLUTTON, B.A., Cantab, F.R.C.S. Numerous Coloured Plates and Illustrations, 8vo, strongly bound in flexible leather, 1l. 8s.

TAUCHNITZ'S English Editions of German Authors. Each volume, cloth flexible, 2s.; or sewed, 1s. 6d. (Catalogues post free on application.)

* *See also* Rose Library.

Tauchnitz (B.) German and English Dictionary. Paper, 1s. cloth, 1s. 6d. ; roan, 2s.

—— *French and English.* Paper, 1s. 6d. ; cloth, 2s ; roan, 2s. 6d.

—— *Italian and English.* Paper, 1s. 6d. ; cloth, 2s. ; roan, 2s. 6d.

—— *Spanish and English.* Paper, 1s. 6d. ; cloth, 2s. ; roan, 2s. 6d.

—— *New Testament.* Cloth, 2s. ; gilt, 2s. 6d.

The Telephone. An Account of the Phenomena of Electricity, Magnetism, and Sound, as Involved in its Action ; with Directions for Making a Speaking Telephone. By Prof. A. E. DOLBEAR, Author of "The Art of Projecting," &c. Second Edition, with an Appendix Descriptive of Prof. BELL's Present Instrument. 130 pp., with 19 Illustrations, 1s.

Tennyson's May Queen. Choicely Illustrated from designs by the Hon. Mrs. BOYLE. Crown 8vo (*See* Choice Series), 2s. 6d.

Textbook (A) of Harmony. For the Use of Schools and Students. By the late CHARLES EDWARD HORSLEY. Revised for the Press by WESTLEY RICHARDS and W. H. CALCOTT. Small post 8vo, cloth extra, 3s. 6d.

Thebes, and its Five Greater Temples. See ABNEY.

Thomson (J.) The Straits of Malacca, Indo-China, and China ; or, Ten Years' Travels, Adventures, and Residence Abroad. By J. THOMSON, F.R.G.S., Author of "Illustrations of China and its People." Upwards of 60 Woodcuts. Demy 8vo, cloth extra, 21s.

Thorne (E.) The Queen of the Colonies ; or, Queensland as I saw it. 1 vol., with Map, 6s.

Through the Dark Continent : The Sources of the Nile ; Around the Great Lakes, and down the Congo. By HENRY M. STANLEY. 2 vols., demy 8vo, containing 150 Full-page and other Illustrations, 2 Portraits of the Author, and 10 Maps, 42s. Sixth Thousand.

—— *Map to the above.* Size 34 by 56 inches, showing, on a large scale, Stanley's recent Great Discoveries in Central Africa. The First Map in which the Congo was ever correctly traced. Mounted, in case, 1l. 1s.

" One of the greatest geographical discoveries of the age."—*Spectator.*

" Mr. Stanley has penetrated the very heart of the mystery. . . . He has opened up a perfectly virgin region, never before, so far as known, visited by a white man."—*Times.*

To the Arctic Regions and Back in Six Weeks. By Captain A. W. M. CLARK KENNEDY (late of the Coldstream Guards). With Illustrations and Maps. 8vo, cloth, 15s.

Tour of the Prince of Wales in India. See RUSSELL.

Trollope (A.) Harry Heathcote of Gangoil. A Story of Bush Life in Australia. With Graphic Illustrations. Small post, cloth, 5s.

Turkistan. Notes of a Journey in the Russian Provinces of Central Asia and the Khanates of Bokhara and Kokand. By EUGENE SCHUYLER, Secretary to the American Legation, St. Petersburg. Numerous Illustrations. 2 vols, 8vo, cloth extra, 5th Edition, 2l. 2s.

Two Americas ; being an Account of Sport and Travel, with Notes on Men and Manners in North and South America. By Sir ROSE PRICE, Bart. 1 vol., demy 8vo, with Illustrations, cloth extra, 2nd Edition, 18s.

Two Friends. By LUCIEN BIART, Author of "Adventures of a Young Naturalist," "My Rambles in the New World," &c. Small post 8vo, numerous Illustrations, 7s. 6d.

Two Supercargoes (The) ; or, Adventures in Savage Africa. By W. H. G. KINGSTON. Square imperial 16mo, cloth extra, 7s. 6d. Numerous Full-page Illustrations.

VANDENHOFF (George, M.A.). See "Art of Reading Aloud."

———— *Clerical Assistant.* Fcap., 3s. 6d.

———— *Ladies' Reader (The).* Fcap., 5s.

Verne's (Jules) Works. Translated from the French, with from 50 to 100 Illustrations. Each cloth extra, gilt edges—

Large post 8vo, price 10s. 6d. each—

1. Fur Country.
2. Twenty Thousand Leagues under the Sea.
3. From the Earth to the Moon, and a Trip round It.
4. Michael Strogoff, the Courier of the Czar.
5. Hector Servadac.
6. Dick Sands, the Boy Captain.

Imperial 16mo, price 7s. 6d. each—

1. Five Weeks in a Balloon.
2. Adventures of Three Englishmen and Three Russians in South Africa.
3. Around the World in Eighty Days.
4. A Floating City, and the Blockade Runners.
5. Dr. Ox's Experiment, Master Zacharius, A Drama in the Air, A Winter amid the Ice, &c.
6. The Survivors of the "Chancellor."
7. Dropped from the Clouds.
8. Abandoned.
9. Secret of the Island.
10. The Child of the Cavern.

The Mysterious Island. 3 vols., 22s. 6d. One volume, with some of the Illustrations, cloth, gilt edges, 10s. 6d.

Verne's (Jules) Works, continued:—

The following Cheaper Editions are issued with a few of the Illustrations, in paper wrapper, price 1s.; cloth gilt, 2s. each.

1. **Adventures of Three Englishmen and Three Russians in South Africa.**
2. **Five Weeks in a Balloon.**
3. **A Floating City.**
4. **The Blockade Runners.**
5. **From the Earth to the Moon.**
6. **Around the Moon.**
7. **Twenty Thousand Leagues under the Sea.** Vol. I.
8. —— Vol. II. The two parts in one, cloth, gilt, 3s. 6d.
9. **Around the World in Eighty Days.**
10. **Dr. Ox's Experiment, and Master Zacharius.**
11. **Martin Paz, the Indian Patriot.**
12. **A Winter amid the Ice.**
13. **The Fur Country.** Vol. I.
14. —— Vol. II. Both parts in one, cloth gilt, 3s. 6d.
15. **Survivors of the "Chancellor."** Vol. I.
16. —— Vol. II. Both volumes in one, cloth, gilt edges, 3s. 6d.

Viardot (Louis). See " Painters of all Schools."

WALLER (Rev. C. H.) The Names on the Gates of Pearl, and other Studies. By the Rev. C. H. WALLER, M.A. Crown 8vo, cloth extra, 6s.

—— *A Grammar and Analytical Vocabulary of the Words in* the Greek Testament. Compiled from Brüder's Concordance. For the use of Divinity Students and Greek Testament Classes. By the Rev. C. H. WALLER, M.A., late Scholar of University College, Oxford, Tutor of the London College of Divinity, St. John's Hall, Highbury. Part I., The Grammar. Small post 8vo, cloth, 2s. 6d. Part II. The Vocabulary, 2s. 6d.

—— *Adoption and the Covenant.* Some Thoughts on Confirmation. Super-royal 16mo, cloth limp, 2s. 6d.

War in Bulgaria: a Narrative of Personal Experiences. By LIEUTENANT-GENERAL VALENTINE BAKER PASHA. Together with a Description and Plan of the Works constructed by him for the Defence of Constantinople. Also Maps and Plans of Battles. 2 vols., demy 8vo, cloth extra, 2l. 2s.

Warner (C. D.) My Summer in a Garden. Rose Library, 1s.

—— *Back-log Studies.* Boards, 1s. 6d.; cloth, 2s.

—— *In the Wilderness.* Rose Library, 1s.

—— *Mummies and Moslems.* 8vo, cloth, 12s.

Weaving. See " History and Principles."

Westropp (H. M.) A Manual of Precious Stones and Antique Gems. By HODDER M. WESTROPP, Author of "The Traveller's Art Companion," "Pre-Historic Phases," &c. Numerous Illustrations. Small post 8vo, cloth extra, 6s.

Whitney (Mrs. A. D. T.) The Gayworthys. Cloth, 3s. 6d.

———— *Faith Gartney.* Small post 8vo, 3s. 6d. Cheaper Editions, 1s. 6d. and 2s.

———— *Real Folks.* 12mo, crown, 3s. 6d.

———— *Hitherto.* Small post 8vo, 3s. 6d. and 2s. 6d.

———— *Sights and Insights.* 3 vols., crown 8vo, 31s. 6d.

———— *Summer in Leslie Goldthwaite's Life.* Cloth, 3s. 6d.

———— *The Other Girls.* Small post 8vo, cloth extra, 3s. 6d.

———— *We Girls.* Small post 8vo, 3s. 6d.; Cheap Edition, 1s. 6d. and 2s.

Wikoff (H.) The Four Civilizations of the World. An Historical Retrospect. Crown 8vo, cloth, 12s.

Wills, A Few Hints on Proving, without Professional Assistance. By a PROBATE COURT OFFICIAL. 5th Edition, revised with Forms of Wills, Residuary Accounts, &c. Fcap. 8vo, cloth limp, 1s.

Wilson (H. Schültz). See " Alpine Ascents and Adventures."

With Axe and Rifle on the Western Prairies. By W. H. G. KINGSTON. With numerous Illustrations, square crown 8vo, cloth extra, gilt, 7s. 6d.

Woolsey (C. D., LL.D.) Introduction to the Study of International Law; designed as an Aid in Teaching and in Historical Studies. Reprinted from the last American Edition, and at a much lower price. Crown 8vo, cloth extra, 8s. 6d.

Words of Wellington: Maxims and Opinions, Sentences and Reflections of the Great Duke, gathered from his Despatches, Letters, and Speeches (Bayard Series). 2s. 6d.

World of Comets. By A. GUILLEMIN, Author of "The Heavens." Translated and edited by JAMES GLAISHER, F.R.S. 1 vol., super-royal 8vo, with numerous Woodcut Illustrations, and 3 Chromo-lithographs, cloth extra, 31s. 6d.
  "The mass of information collected in the volume is immense, and the treatment of the subject is so purely popular, that none need be deterred from a perusal of it."—*British Quarterly Review.*

Wreck of the Grosvenor. By W. CLARK RUSSELL. 6s. Third and Cheaper Edition.

XENOPHON'S Anabasis; or, Expedition of Cyrus. A
Literal Translation, chiefly from the Text of Dindorff, by GEORGE
B. WHEELER. Books I to III. Crown 8vo, boards, 2*s.*

—— *Books I. to VII.* Boards, 3*s.* 6*d.* .

YOUNG (J. F.) Five Weeks in Greece. Crown 8vo, 10*s.* 6*d.*

London.

SAMPSON LOW, MARSTON, SEARLE, & RIVINGTON,
CROWN BUILDINGS, 188, FLEET STREET.

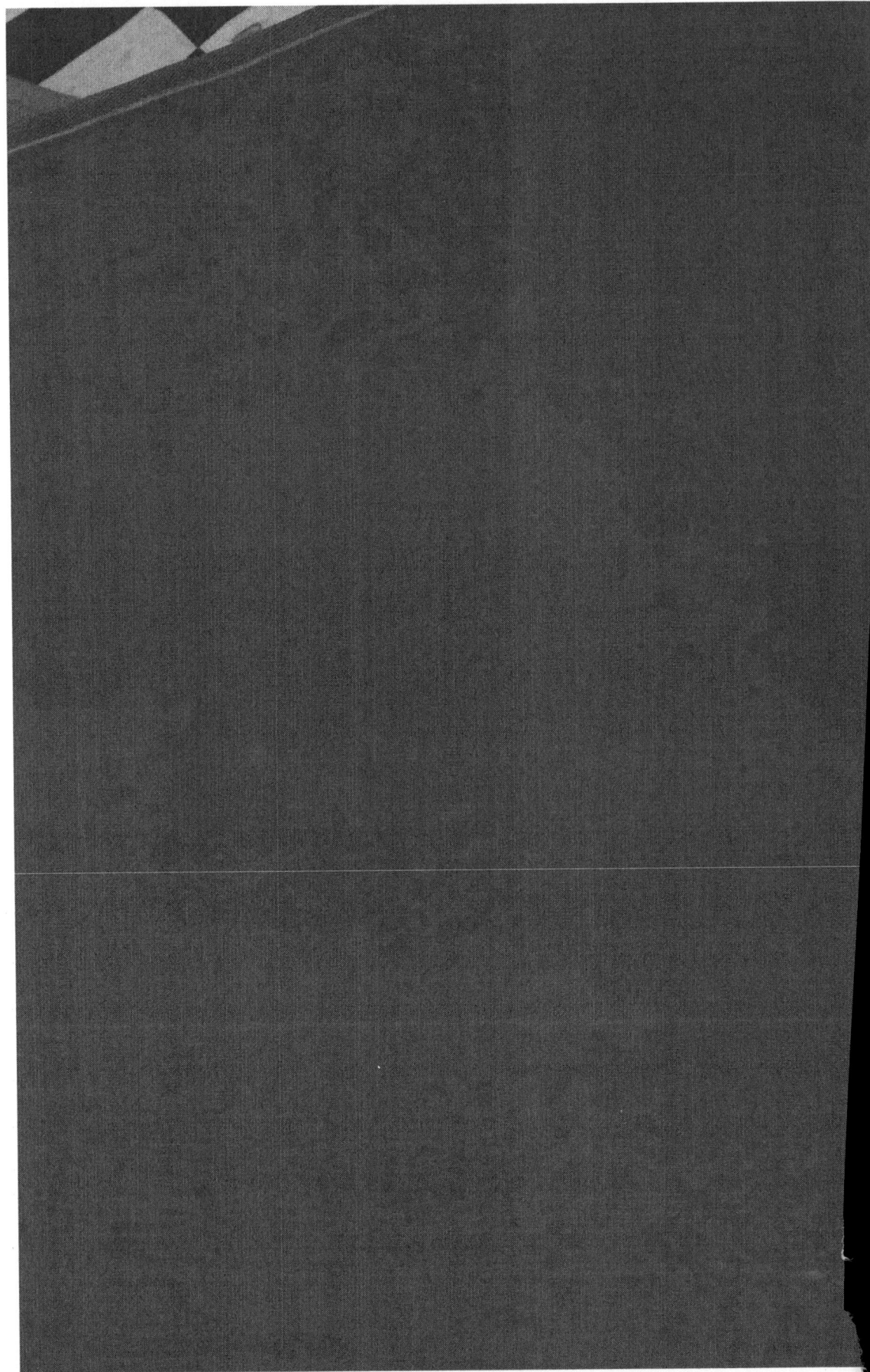